MOTORCYCLIST'S LEGAL HANDBOOK

How to handle legal situations from the mundane to the insane

PAT HAHN

motorbooks

First published in 2011 by Motorbooks, an imprint of MBI Publishing Company,
400 First Avenue North, Suite 300, Minneapolis, MN 55401 USA

Library of Congress Cataloging-in-Publication Data

Hahn, Pat, 1969-
 Motorcyclist's legal handbook : how to handle legal situations from the mundane to the
insane / Pat Hahn.
    p. cm.
 ISBN 978-0-7603-4023-3 (softbound)
 1. Motorcycles—Law and legislation--United States. 2. Motorcycles—Law and
legislation—United States—States. 3. Motorcyclists—United States—Handbooks, manuals,
etc. I. Title.
 KF2220.M6H34 2011
 343.7309'44—dc23

                                                                      2011032810

Editor: Steve Casper
Design Manager: Kou Lor
Designer: Simon Larkin
Layout: Chris Fayers
Cover designer: Rob Johnson, Toprotype, Inc.

Photo Credits:
All images provided by the author, with the exception of:
American Suzuki: pages 25, 50, 92, 139
Darryl and Lori Cannon, Killboy.com: pages 6, 135, 136, 141, 197, 199, 235
iStock.com: front cover
Kawasaki Motors Corporation: pages frontis, 18, 77, 177
Polaris Industries, Inc.: pages 20, 72, 105, 118
Shutterstock: pages 17, 22, 26, 30, 35, 38, 45, 47, 53, 74, 80, 85, 87, 90, 96, 109, 122
Yamaha Motor Corporation: pages 9, 85, 113, back cover

Printed in China

10 9 8 7 6 5 4 3 2 1

CONTENTS

Introduction

The chief goal of this book is to help motorcycle enthusiasts understand how to keep their driving records clean.

A clean driving record is a key element to enjoyable motorcycling that many riders overlook. Understandably, avoiding administrative hassles isn't on anyone's priority list, but when dings on your record pile up, they have a way of separating motorcyclists from the activity they love. A traffic stop is embarrassing and time consuming, and it takes the fun out of an otherwise great day of riding. Paying for something like a speeding ticket (known as "entertainment tax" in some circles) cuts into the fun of spending money on tires, gas, food, and those cool little hotels in the mountains.

Allowing too many traffic convictions to pile up on your record has a way of taking all the fun out of riding. You may end up being forced to park your bike for weeks or months because you're no longer legal in the eyes of the law. It doesn't have to be that way.

An added bonus for riders who steer clear of troubles with the law is that they'll be much more likely to come home in one piece. No matter what we may think about any particular motorcycle regulation, most of the laws on the books are designed primarily for the safety of the riders themselves, and following them might mean they get to enjoy many more decades in the saddle.

This book aims to turn your driving record into the least of your worries—which it should be.

First, you should learn how to stay unnoticed. This is most important. In *Jurassic Park*, the way to escape the jaws of *T. rex* was simply to stay put. The big monster's eyes weren't good enough to distinguish an object from the background unless it was moving. Getting spotted by law enforcement (or not) works the same way. If you can become indistinguishable from the background noise of other traffic, the predator will find more obvious and satisfying prey.

Next, you have to know the laws. The oldest saying in the municipal codebook is "ignorance is no excuse." And of course that is still true today. But it can get really tricky because laws pertaining to motorcyclists vary from state to state. However, there is a set of general regulations that is in fact virtually identical in every state. Some of these "universal" laws were adopted way back when and never changed, and there are some standard laws that states enacted to solve bigger problems; then there are some idiosyncratic laws that stand out from the rest.

Certain things are not tolerated anywhere (such as passing a school bus while it's dropping off children). Other things are pretty much tolerated everywhere (such as roaring around with loud pipes) even though the laws are pretty clear that you're not supposed to be doing that.

Sooner or later it seems that everyone gets stopped. If you want to keep your record clean, it's very important that you know what to do (and what not to do) when you're on the side of the road chatting with a man with a gun.

Only one in 10 Americans is a motorcycle rider; to the other nine, we're a mystery. I'd estimate that two or three in 10 cops are motorcycle riders, but to the rest of them we're a mystery as well—and our vehicles of choice can go really, really fast, and they look really, really dangerous to nonriders. A smart rider looking to preserve his or her privilege to drive is wise to understand this dilemma and take responsibility for defusing the tension of a roadside stop.

No matter how well you stay below the radar, how well you know the laws, and how well behaved you are when you are stopped, chances are you're someday going to end up with a traffic ticket in your hand. But just because the cop hands it to you (and you take it) doesn't mean you have to simply roll over and pay it. Riders interested in keeping their records clean consider a ticket only a written notice that someone, somewhere, is accusing them of doing something unsafe or illegal. It doesn't mean they actually *did* something unsafe or illegal. It's up to the accuser to *prove* a rider did something unsafe or illegal. We're innocent until proven guilty, and the onus of proof is on the accuser. Nine out of 10 or more drivers in this country just knuckle down and pay their tickets, which makes it really easy for law enforcement to justify writing them. But if you're motivated to keep your driving privileges intact, you'll learn how to

stand up for yourself, appear in court, and fight your traffic ticket to keep your record clean.

In the State-by-State Guide, finer details of individual state laws will help you understand what's tolerated in any given state—yours or one you happen to be traveling through—and what's not. But there are many other tidbits included to help you plan your riding strategy and stay below the radar.

I dug up some statistics to help rank states based on how much room there is to ride and enjoy ourselves, how many cops are patrolling the roads, and how bad car drivers are at sharing the road with motorcyclists. I interviewed hundreds of motorcycle riders, state administrators, and law enforcers, and I reviewed all the state driver manuals, motorcycle manuals, statute websites, and other resources to get an idea of what it's like to ride in that state and what the relative importance is of each of these criteria. I pooled them all into a spreadsheet and spit out a ranking of the best states and the worst states to ride in as far as being safe and the chances of not getting ticketed, based on the following:

- **Population density**
- **Law enforcement density**
- **Percentage of fatal multi-vehicle motorcycle crashes to all crashes**

Note that I did not try to include the quality of the roads or the quality of riding in the state rideability index. As one rider, I can't possibly quantify states by how many twisty, scenic roads they have. A state could have a very high rideability rank and have boring, straight, flat roads. Some riders prefer this. On the other hand, a state could have a low rank but be more fun than a barrel of monkeys to ride—for whatever reason. You'll have to look at a roadmap and hobbyist websites and decide that for yourself. But here is what the rankings are actually based on.

POPULATION DENSITY

This is not specifically a legal paradigm, but sparsely populated areas have a whole different riding environment from those that are densely populated when it comes to traffic and law enforcement stops. The assumption made is that the lower the population density, the better the riding. Rural areas have fewer folks to share the road with, lots of room to explore, and fewer slowdowns. Of course there are exceptions, but in general motorcycle riders prefer the backcountry. If you prefer built-up areas with lots of intersections, driveways, and other traffic, you might disagree with the state rideability rankings.

LAW ENFORCEMENT DENSITY

If your goal is to keep your record clean, the fewer individuals out there who have the power to tarnish it, the better. The implementation of law enforcement

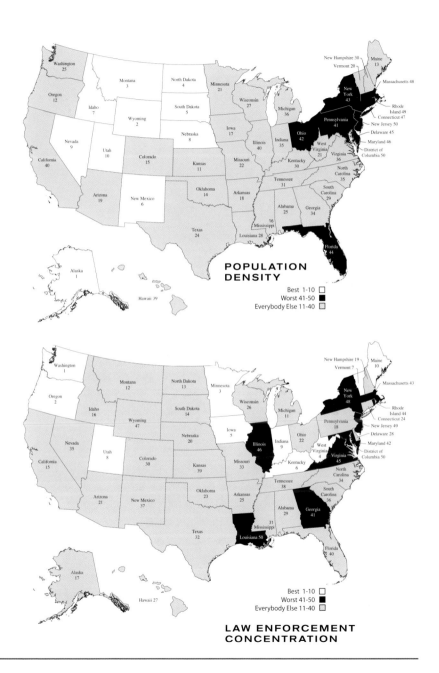

POPULATION DENSITY

Best 1-10 ☐
Worst 41-50 ■
Everybody Else 11-40 ☐

LAW ENFORCEMENT CONCENTRATION

Best 1-10 ☐
Worst 41-50 ■
Everybody Else 11-40 ☐

throughout the country takes no standard shape or size and is therefore hard to quantify. For the purposes of this book, I looked at U.S. Department of Justice census data to get an idea of the manpower that states put into highway safety. The census estimates the number of sworn officers per 100,000 citizens—I compared those numbers only. The number of officers by itself is understandably not a good gauge, but the relative density of law enforcement from state to state can help a rider make decisions and prepare. The roads of some states are heavy with traffic enforcement. Others are relatively light. The individual results might surprise you—each state's ranking is noted in the State-by-State Guide. The state rankings were written on the assumption that the lower the ratio of law enforcement officers to individual citizens, the better your chances are for not getting pulled over.

MULTI-VEHICLE TO SINGLE-VEHICLE MOTORCYCLE CRASH RATIO

You can't analyze a state's rideability without a nod to the local car drivers and how they handle sharing the road with motorcycles. Either they get bikes or they don't. Across the nation, when motorcyclists receive fatal injuries in a wreck, the ratio of multi-vehicle motorcycle crashes to single-vehicle motorcycle crashes is, believe it or not, around 50/50. That means that motorcycle riders are at least 50 percent responsible for their own survival. (If you buy into the argument that in a multi-vehicle crash, both drivers share the responsibility equally, motorcycle riders are then awarded 75 percent of the responsibility for their own safety.)

Even though the majority of states hover near that 50/50 mark, the ratio varies wildly from the lowest ratio of 37/63 (Montana) to the highest of 75/25 (Washington, D.C.). In other words, in the District of Columbia, out of every 100 motorcycle crashes, 75 involve another moving vehicle and 25 are motorcycle only.

The Multi-Vehicle to Single-Vehicle Motorcycle Crash Ratio is a reflection of the combination of local attitude, motorist awareness, population density, and traffic patterns and exposure, but it still felt right to use it to establish a state rideability rank. For example, you wouldn't want to visit a state based just on its law enforcement density only to find out quickly (and painfully) that its drivers treat

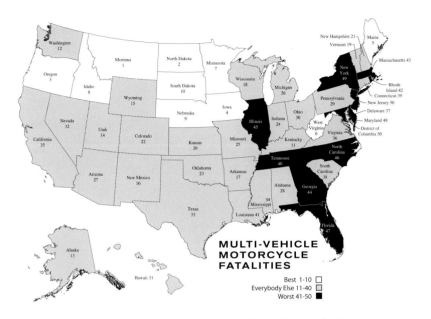

MULTI-VEHICLE
MOTORCYCLE
FATALITIES

Best 1-10 ☐
Everybody Else 11-40 ☐
Worst 41-50 ■

stop signs and right-of-way rules only informally. The data used for this measure were official, national (NHTSA) crash-type data from the past five years.

But the relative importance of these three criteria is not equal among motorcycle riders. What's important to one, I found out, was not important to another. Some riders don't care about law enforcement density, but they do care about drunk football fans driving pickup trucks on curvy roads in Wisconsin. Other riders don't care about other drivers, but the number of them makes a difference to their enjoyment of the road, which is why some folks choose to live in places like Idaho. Every person interviewed ranked population density, law enforcement density, and the ratio of multi-vehicle crashes to single-vehicle crashes from 1 to 10, 1 being most important and 10 being least important. To get the truest rideability rankings, I added them up, averaged them out, and applied them to the statistics to give each measure a relative importance in the final rideability rankings for the states.

Motorist awareness of motorcycles, as evidenced by multi-vehicle crash data, was most important to riders, with an average rating of 3.8 out of 10. That is, when asked how important other drivers' idiocy was to their riding enjoyment, most riders ranked this highest. Population density was next most important, with an average of 4.4 out of 10. Law enforcement density was last, at 5.7. The State-by-State Guide directly reflects this: Under each state, you can get a general idea of how intelligent car drivers are compared to the amount of space you have to work with and the number of cops assigned to traffic duty—all neatly rolled up into the rideability ranking.

In Part II of this book each state is assigned a rideability rank at the beginning of each section. Based on the indexes described above, the 10 best and the 10 worst states to ride in are as follows:

Best	Worst
1. Montana	41. Louisiana
2. North Dakota	42. Rhode Island
3. Oregon	43. Massachusetts
4. Iowa	44. Georgia
5. Maine	45. Illinois
6. West Virginia	46. North Carolina
7. Minnesota	47. Florida
8. Idaho	48. Maryland
9. Nebraska	49. New York
10. South Dakota	50. New Jersey and District of Columbia

A fourth measure of a state's rideability was supposed to be "tone of law enforcement." In different regions of the country, individual states, and even subregions and local jurisdictions, the tone of law enforcement toward motorcyclists can vary widely. In some states, a rider would have to break a dozen laws simultaneously in front of the local cop shop even to raise an eyebrow; in others, just having your wallet attached to a chain arouses suspicion. Or so I thought.

In my initial interviews, I assigned four primary attitudes that law enforcement could have toward motorcycle riders.

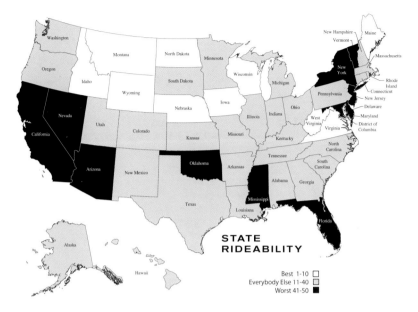

STATE RIDEABILITY

Best 1-10 ☐
Everybody Else 11-40 ☐
Worst 41-50 ■

- Indifferent: motorcyclists are generally ignored by law enforcement
- Businesslike: law enforcement officers treat motorcyclists just like any other motorist
- Enthusiastic: those in law enforcement actively seek out opportunities to stop motorcyclists
- Aggressive: motorcyclists are often singled out for special attention

Amazingly, only a handful of respondents identified law enforcement in their state as anything but "businesslike." A few riders, apparently hell-bent on flaunting the laws at every turn, of course made their points about the drill-sergeant cops out to spoil their fun. But the overwhelming majority agreed that law enforcement officers are just doing their jobs, and if you get a ticket it's because you probably earned it, not because they're trying to meet a quota or they have a "thing" against motorcyclists. This is important to keep in mind: Even though your perception may be that you were singled out and treated unfairly, such incidents are the exception, not the rule.

Some states are very aggressive with enforcing such things as helmet laws, speeding, exhaust noise, etc. But the riders who live there rarely perceive it as being aggressive. Even the states that I know—from experience, talking to their state highway safety offices—to be decidedly aggressive from an organizational/government perspective were still not identified as such by the riders there. Therefore, I did not include this figure in the state rankings. Even so, I still included "tone of law enforcement" in the State-by-State Guide because there were a few strong enthusiastic and/or aggressive showings that riders should be aware of.

The information in this book is meant for reference and travel preparation and to increase the reader's knowledge for riding within the law throughout the country. It does not constitute legal advice. Each legal dispute entails unique facts, and there may be hidden effects, such as employment, licensing, or immigration consequences, arising even from a petty misdemeanor. A legal infraction today might have consequences in the future, such as reducing the relief available if you have another legal problem. Depending on the rider, one's personality, and circumstances, a run-in with the law could have serious implications. If you have any doubts about your legal rights, speak to a competent lawyer experienced in the subject matter.

Please note that while this book often addresses speed limits, and issues such as where speed limits are more or less rigorously enforced, I am, of course, not encouraging anyone to speed or otherwise break the law. The best way to ride long, safe, and happy is to look out for yourself and the people you ride with, minimize risks, and take nothing for granted.

Information for this book has been gathered from state, city, and county government websites and publications, motorist and motorcyclist organizations, and interviews with motorists, motorcycle riders, and law enforcement officers. The author and publisher assume no responsibility for the way readers interpret the content or use the material in this book.

Note that this book does not tell you how to obtain your motorcycle license. It is assumed that you are already a licensed rider. Each state listing, however, includes Web links to that state's licensing authority or department of motor vehicles, which normally provides licensing information.

The Basics

This book is basically divided into two primary sections; Part I details the best ways to keep your riding record spotless, as well as ensuring a safe ride, while Part II is a quick and handy reference guide to the various rules and regulations one might encounter while crossing state lines on a cross-country tour.

This first section of the book begins with a chapter on how to stay "under the radar" when you hit the road on your motorcycle. Many seemingly small things may cause law enforcement officials to take an extra-careful look at you. Avoiding those behaviors can greatly decrease your chances of getting pulled over.

The second chapter deciphers all the various laws and regulations that are in place for street bikers and makes each one easier to understand. Many are broad-based and cross state lines, but some rules and regs are very state-specific. Having a good handle on exactly what these laws mean to motorcycle riders (as well as law enforcement officials) will help keep your record clean.

In the third chapter, riders will learn the correct way to respond when getting pulled over by a cop. Having solid knowledge of these tips and techniques may very well make the difference between getting a ticket or getting a warning. How you act and respond when getting pulled over could also determine the final outcome of a courtroom appearance, either for the good or the bad.

The final chapter details the various steps a rider can take to keep his or her record clean, as well as decrease or eliminate any fines if he or she does happen to get a ticket. There are, in fact, several different legal strategies that many riders may never be aware of that in the end can save them a lot of time and money if they happen to "get nicked by the man."

1

Staying Under the Radar

The smartest and easiest way to keep your driving record clean is to avoid drawing attention to yourself by your driving behavior, your bike, or your equipment. In other words, keep your head down.

Most riders enjoy sticking out like a sore thumb in traffic. In traffic, it's actually a good strategy. Being conspicuous is a good thing for your life and limb. But when traveling in rural areas or out of state, like most riding enthusiasts prefer, sticking out too much can slow you down by getting pulled over. Riders can employ several strategies to skate by relatively unnoticed by law enforcement.

SPEED LIMITS

Speeding is the most common reason a driver draws the attention of law enforcement. It's obvious, because you're moving faster than the other traffic or faster than what is typical. It's measurable, based on devices such as Radar or Lidar (a device, similar in operation to radar, that uses pulses of laser light to analyze atmospheric phenomena—speeding). Law enforcement officers can learn through both training and experience how to judge whether or not a vehicle is speeding. Speed is quantifiable, meaning an officer can tell you (or a judge) exactly how fast you were traveling and exactly what the limit is on that stretch of road with reasonably good accuracy and reliability. And it's predictable:

> LEGAL BRIEFS: **Speeding is the most common reason a driver draws the attention of law enforcement.**

Everybody exceeds the speed limit at one time or another, half of us exceed it every day, and a great many of us exceed it by a lot—except the sweet little old lady who only uses her Buick to get to church and back on Sunday. (I've got news for you: Even she speeds once in awhile.) For law enforcement, nabbing drivers and citing them with speeding is as easy as shooting ducks in the bathtub.

HEAD DOWN TIP #1

As a rule, to keep your record clean, always keep your speed at or below the posted limit. Well, duh. If there are other vehicles, flowing with them is usually a good approximation of the maximum speed. While in open spaces, glance regularly at your speedometer when it's safe to do so (e.g., not during a sharp turn).

No matter what the limit is on any given road, basic speed law in every state requires drivers to drive at a speed that is reasonable and prudent for existing

conditions—a speed at which a reasonable person would travel in the same conditions. This does not mean it's ever okay or permissible to travel faster than the posted limit, even though it may seem reasonable based on the conditions. Confounding conditions include weather, road surface, driving environment (city, suburb, rural, construction, school zone, roadside crash, etc.), traffic volume, traffic speed, and the type and/or condition of your vehicle and any load you may be hauling. Simply following the letter of the law and riding at the posted limit can still get you a ticket in poor driving conditions, so consider it a maximum limit under ideal conditions.

HEAD DOWN TIP #2

You can get a speeding ticket even if you're at or below the posted limit.

Reasonable and Prudent: Sometimes, especially as a rider, sticking to the posted limit makes you an obstacle (or target, with a bull's-eye on your back) in traffic. There will be times when, for your own safety, you're better off traveling at the same speed as the prevailing traffic, even if the traffic is exceeding the speed limit. Note, however, that giving the cop who stopped you the old line "I was traveling at the speed of the rest of the traffic" will rarely get you out of a ticket. If the prevailing speed on a road is faster than you're comfortable riding, then find an alternate route.

Different jurisdictions and regions have different approaches to speeding enforcement. As a basic rule, when you are within a couple hours of a population center, the farther away from the city you are, the less likely you are to get away with a whole lot. (When you're way out in the boondocks in the Great Plains, desert, and mountains, the opposite is true.) In the city, the ratio of drivers to law enforcement officers is much, much higher than it is in the sticks. Therefore, the speed limit that is technically enforced as reasonable and prudent is much higher in the city than in the areas surrounding small towns.

In built-up areas, traffic enforcement maintains a flashing red and blue presence to keep people on their guard and slow down traffic overall. Traffic enforcement is not necessarily meant to slow down individuals . . . although there are always exceptions for those who are just asking for it. For example, if traffic is cruising along on an urban interstate loop at 10 mph over the limit, you will get noticed if you pass everyone at 15 over. Out in less populated areas, it's less likely that enforcement will slow down traffic as a whole and more likely that it's an individual matter: This individual is driving too fast; he therefore gets a roadside chat about slowing down.

Speeds go up on metropolitan highways, and the speed at which normal traffic travels is at least 5 to 10 mph higher than the posted limit during high-volume times, such as during the day. At night, when the happy-hour crowd or all-night-drinking crowd hits the road, the acceptable speed limit goes down quite a bit, especially for law enforcement. But the reality is that there's no way they can get everyone when everyone's traveling at the same illegal speed. Like predators selecting one likely beast from the herd, cops have to choose their prey. Don't do anything to stand out from the crowd.

HEAD DOWN TIP #3

On highways in built-up or metropolitan areas during daylight and rush hours, ride no faster than the prevailing traffic—or if you must, ride only slightly faster.

HEAD DOWN TIP #4

On highways in built-up or metropolitan areas during darkness hours, ride no faster than the prevailing traffic or 4 mph over the limit, whichever is lower.

Suburban and nearby rural town highways and surface streets tolerate a lot less speeding than city highways. In fact, they often tolerate none of it. The driver-to-cop ratio is quite a bit smaller and the crime that city cops have to deal with is not as prevalent. Plan to keep your speed at the posted limit unless there is a real push from other traffic to travel faster.

HEAD DOWN TIP #5

In rural towns in speed zones of 25 to 30 mph or less, keep your speed below the legal limit.

There are a couple other considerations for when you really need to keep your rate of travel on the down-low. On 55-mph state highways, U.S. highways, and interstates (for example, State Highway 77; U.S. 61; Interstate 40 or I-40), law enforcement, particularly the state police, have a much greater presence—and a far more enthusiastic approach to keeping speeds down. Many travelers are not from that area, and when people make mistakes at those high speeds, the wreckage is dramatic.

Keep your speed to the posted limit or that of the prevailing traffic. If you're going to speed on these types of highways in these areas, it's best to identify a rabbit (fast driver) traveling at or above the speed you want to travel, let him get ahead of you by a half mile, and then pick up your pace and keep him a half mile in front of you at all times.

On the other hand, 55-mph posted, county-numbered, or lettered roads (River Road; County Highway 30; County Road MM) are used primarily by locals. They're also usually the best roads for motorcycle riding. It is a happy coincidence that they are noticeably less populated by law enforcement, especially those state police who are highly efficient in nabbing speeders and writing tickets on the major highways. The side roads are left to the local governments to patrol, and there is far fewer of them.

The existing lore is that drivers are safe at anything less than 5 mph over, that 9 over will get you noticed but not necessarily stopped, and that anything 10 mph or

more above the limit will probably get you nicked. However, these 55-mph-limit roads almost always have a reduced speed through town, so there will be multiple opportunities for speed traps every time the speed limit drops. On your way into town, you'll see a warning that lets you know that the speed limit decreases in a quarter mile. Roll off the throttle now. That first sign that says 40 or 45 is your first opportunity to screw up at 5 to 10 over the limit. Shortly, the limit will drop to 30 or 35, and then 25, and every step of the way is a chance to miscalculate your deceleration and piss off the local cop. When you know you're heading into town, and back out again, assume that the speed will drop to 25 and plan accordingly. Slow early and keep your speed to 3 to 5 mph below the limit.

LEGAL BRIEFS: **Most riders agree that you can get away with 4 mph over the limit pretty easily, 9 over the limit without too much trouble, but beyond that you're asking to get stopped.**

Another very general and admittedly arbitrarily noted difference between major highways and local roads is the attitude and experience of the law enforcement officers. County and state cops are much more consistently businesslike and unmoved by personal dilemmas in their manner of stopping and citing motorists and motorcyclists. Local police officers are generally presumed to be more informal, familiar, friendly, and malleable when it comes to whether or not your stop ends with a ticket or a warning. However, they can also be mavericks and a lot harder on a rider for minor infractions than a statey would be in the same situation.

HEAD DOWN TIP #6
Keep to the speed limit on major rural highways unless there's a lot of fast-moving traffic or you have a rabbit a half mile ahead running interference for you.

HEAD DOWN TIP #7
Law enforcement density and intensity drops when you're on named, numbered, or lettered local roads. If you can, build your road trips around roads like these—they're much more fun anyway.

HEAD DOWN TIP #8
When the speed starts dropping from 55 mph on your way into town, slow early and often and plan to travel at 20 mph shortly.

Advisory Speed Limits: On many curves, and certainly all the best curves or combinations, there is usually a black and yellow sign with an arrow to warn you and give you an idea of what's coming up. Many times, beneath that sign, will be another black and yellow sign with an advisory speed limit. This speed limit is almost always lower than the prevailing limit—the speed limit that applied to the straightaway you were just enjoying.

Advisory speed limit signs are just that—advisory. They do not carry the weight of law. The speed limit is still what you last saw on the black-on-white regulatory sign a while back. The advisory speed limit is set as a courtesy to ordinary drivers, a recommendation of a safer speed at which to attempt that corner. A rider is completely within her rights to take that corner at the posted straightaway speed if her machine and skills are up to the task. This also assumes that conditions are such that it is reasonable for you to do so. If you're in mountain fog or morning mist, holding 55 through a curve may be neither reasonable nor safe.

LEGAL BRIEFS: **Even what you do with your hands and feet (stretching, standing, shaking out a clutch cramp—you name it) is grounds for extra attention.**

Although an advisory speed limit is not a law, law enforcement can write you a ticket for speeding if you have a crash and you were observed traveling above that limit. You can also get pulled over for riding too fast for conditions. If you're being followed by a police officer and you choose to ignore the advisory limits, you're gambling that the cop won't want to waste the time of either of you.

Riding Behavior: Other riding decisions not based on speed can also get you noticed. Wearing an obviously noncompliant beanie helmet in a mandatory helmet state is an invitation for passing cops to find some other reason to pull you over. Passing or overtaking on a two-lane highway tends to draw attention, because on a motorcycle even a modest pass still gets you up to 15 or 20 over the limit in a hurry. Passing in town, especially near a school, school bus, church, or railroad tracks, can also win you a ticket to pay.

Even what you do with your hands and feet (stretching, standing, shaking out a clutch cramp—you name it) is grounds for extra attention. Some states have laws that require both hands on the bars at all times. When there's traffic around, use your model beginner-rider-training behavior and exaggerate how law abiding you are. If you're running a loud pipe, be aware that you can dramatically change the decibel output simply through smart throttle management. This is especially important in quaint little tourist towns where law enforcement officers have a keen ear for loud noises.

LEGAL BRIEFS: **If you're running a loud pipe, be aware that you can dramatically change the decibel output simply through smart throttle management.**

REQUIRED EQUIPMENT:

Keeping your equipment in order is a key element in keeping your head down and avoiding

Your behavior can, at times, increase the likelihood of being stopped.

law enforcement interactions. If your goal is to travel without hassles, be careful when modifying your bike to make it look or sound better.

What's required from state to state varies in the details, but there are certain principles that occur often enough in the rulebooks (though not necessarily ticket books) that they should be considered more or less universal. The same rules apply to most every vehicle, which is why it's often not spelled out specifically for motorcycle riders.

When it comes to a rider's driving record, equipment violations rarely entail demerit points. But they can include significant fines and hassle and open the door to additional citations. Roaring out of town with aftermarket pipes after having a few cold ones at the saloon could open a real can of worms. Many of the equipment requirements by state are included in the State-by-State Guide, but not all. Included with each state's entry are Web links to that state's licensing authority and state statutes for you to chase down on your own as needed.

What's required at a roadside stop and what's required for a state inspection are different. State inspectors have checklists, yardsticks, and specification details that are equivalent to a complete top-to-bottom physical exam, including the "one around the back." Law enforcement officers are not equipment experts, and they generally notice only the most obvious infractions: missing equipment, loud exhaust, illegal plate mount, etc.

HEAD DOWN TIP #9

A well-maintained stock bike is relatively invisible to law enforcement compared to a homemade, custom, or patchwork bike.

AT THE ROADSIDE

Brakes: All states require at least one brake on a motorcycle; a few states require both front and rear brakes. Research for this book has shown that no one, ever, gets ticketed for not having two brakes on a bike in a state that requires two, so those state-by-state requirements have gone unexplored here.

Fenders: Half the states require a rear fender, or both fenders, on your motorcycle. You know those ridiculous plastic fenders that come on motorcycles in the showroom? There's a reason they exist. They're not just to give some new rider a thing to modify with a hacksaw. Their purpose is to prevent the unnecessary spray of mud and rocks around—that is, to "fend" off things kicked up by the tires. Each state entry in the State-by-State Guide will let you know if fenders are required or not.

Handlebars: Many states set limits on handlebar height and condition—they can't be bent and rebent to the point of being laughably weak. Each state entry in the State-by-State Guide that has a law will have information about just how high those handgrips can go.

Headlight: The device should be a white light and have both high- and low-beam capability. States often use language such as "at least one but not more than two" lamps with high and low beam. This doesn't mean to include auxiliaries such as fog and driving lamps, though a few states limit the total number of auxiliaries to four or fewer. About half the states require that the headlamp be used during the daytime. Each state entry in the State-by-State Guide will have information about whether that state requires headlight use during the daytime.

Headlight Modulator: A headlight modulator is a device that pulses the lamp high/low, high/low at a certain rate during the daytime. Conscientious motorcyclists install one of these devices in hopes that it will add to their front-view conspicuity—that other drivers will be more apt to see them before they pull out. (Actually, these riders hope that drivers will sit there and say "Huh?" and watch as the motorcycle goes by before they pull out.) The jury is out on whether or not they actually work, but the riders who have them swear by them.

The bad news is, to the untrained law enforcement eye, it looks an awful lot like a "flashing" (on/off, on/off, not "pulsing") light, which is illegal on nonemergency vehicles. Riders running headlight modulators get stopped all the time for it. The good news is that these devices, if they meet the federal specifications for light intensity and high/low cycle speed (generally anything you can buy off the shelf), are 100 percent legal in every state. It says so right in Federal Motor Vehicle Safety Standards, Title 49, Part 571, Standard 108. Modulators are written in as legal in the vehicle code as an exception to the general laws against civilian vehicles running a flashing light. Many law enforcement officers are not aware of this exception (and won't believe you anyway), but if you have a copy of the FMVSS code that says so, it might get you out of having to make a court appearance.

LEGAL BRIEFS: **The bad news is, to the untrained law enforcement eye, a headlight modulator looks an awful lot like a "flashing" (on/off, on/off, not "pulsing") light, which is illegal on nonemergency vehicles.**

Horn: Every state requires a horn, and it's generally required to be audible from a distance of 200 feet. States almost unanimously prohibit any nonemergency vehicle from running a nonstandard warning device—such as a siren, bell, or whistle—unless it's an antitheft device.

License Plate: States vary in their mounting requirements for exactly where and how the plate is positioned and secured. Some ambitious states, fed up with motorcyclists hiding their plates in hopes of escaping detection, have defined exactly what is expected. In the State-by-State Guide, these states are noted with a "yes" next to "license plate," and extra detail is provided. To be safe in any state, you should have a white light to illuminate the plate. It should be mounted securely to prevent swinging. It should also be mounted horizontally to prevent law enforcement officers from having to cock their heads to one side to read it, and it should be placed so that the face of the plate is flat out facing behind you (no angles). A minor angle is usually okay, but for those who like to mount the plate nearly horizontal to the ground up over the rear tire and under the fender, this can get you nicked for some pretty hefty fines. Most states tolerate a plate mounted sideways at the rear axle, especially if you are from out of state.

Mirrors: Most states require at least one mirror. Many states require two, one on each side of the bike. Each state entry in the State-by-State Guide will note in the "Equipment Requirements" section whether or not a mirror or mirrors are required.

Muffler: Every state requires some sort of device to muffle engine noise. State laws use mostly generic language that specifies that the muffler must be in good working condition and constant operation, and that cutouts, bypasses, and other shade-tree modifications to make it louder are prohibited. Half the states go further in their language to call out additional criteria for what a muffler should or shouldn't be, can or cannot do. A few jurisdictions get downright draconian with their exhaust system requirements. Each state entry in the State-by-State Guide will assume the minimum requirements noted above; under state-at-a-glance laws, "exhaust noise" will say "no," as in there are no special requirements. If a state has language (or enforcement) above and beyond the standard, the exhaust note entry will read "yes" in the at-a-glance state laws, and that section will have additional language if there's more to know about exhaust system requirements.

Operator and Passenger Seats, Footrests, Handholds: Nearly every state calls out the requirement for the operator to ride on a permanent seat. Most states require a permanent passenger seat and footrests if you're carrying a passenger. A few states even specify passenger handholds if you're carrying a passenger. Each state entry in the State-by-State Guide will have information about what the state requires for passenger accommodations.

Reflectors: Requirements vary a bit from state to state, but there is a universal minimum requirement that a bike has at least one red reflector on the rear. Some states call out the requirement for additional amber reflectors on the front and back (sides). Research into this book suggests that no one, ever, gets ticketed

A passenger of the non-human variety provides a great excuse for a cop to pull you over.

for not having the proper reflectors on their bike, so the additional requirements above and beyond the one red rear reflector are not specified.

Speedometer/Odometer: A few states require that one or both of these devices be on the bike and in proper working order. Each state entry in the State-by-State Guide will let you know whether these are required or not.

Taillight, Stop Lamp, Plate Light: Every state more or less requires that the rear lamp should always be red and that the bike includes a stop lamp that lights when the brakes are applied. The lamp needs to be bright enough to be visible from 200 feet. Pretty much every state requires a white light to illuminate the license plate and make it visible at night from 50 feet.

Taillight Modulator: Unlike headlight modulators, taillight modulators are mostly not legal equipment in the United States—but rarely if ever do riders get stopped and ticketed for running one. Almost all police motor officers use them on their bikes. A taillight modulator flashes the stop lamp in various sequences as an added measure to alert sleepy drivers that you're slowing down or stopping. Unfortunately, these devices were not written in to the federal vehicle code as exceptions like headlight modulators were. Technically, they do "flash" the stop lamp on and off. But due to the fact that the stop lamp and tail lamps are so close together (and oftentimes the same bulb), they realistically do pulse high and low. Technically, you can get a citation for running one (as surely some riders have), but most law enforcement officers, when you explain what it does and why— and that you could do the same thing by pumping the brake lever—see it as a legitimate safety device and not a threat to their authority.

Turn Signals: Half the states require electric turn signals on bikes, though many of those states make exceptions for older bikes. Each state entry in the State-by-State Guide will have information about whether or not that state requires electric turn signals. It is important to note that even in those states that do not require turn signals for motorcycles, the requirement that drivers *signal* a turn is nearly universal. Signals generally must be given for at least 100 feet and be visible front and rear from 100 feet, day or night. If you're running without turn signals on your bike, you'd better know how to use hand signals for lefts, rights, and stops. If you're riding at night, you can still get nicked for failing to signal if no one can see it in the dark.

HEAD DOWN TIP #10
Make it a point to exaggerate your hand signals, to the point of being geeky, if you're running a bike without turn signals.

LEGAL BRIEFS: **It is important to note that even in those states that do not require turn signals for motorcycles, the requirement that drivers *signal* a turn is nearly universal.**

CARRYING WEAPONS
The topic of how properly, safely, and legally to carry a firearm on a bike could easily consume another entire book. In fact, it does. *Travelers Guide to the Firearms Laws of the Fifty States* is published annually by the National Rifle Association. There's also a terrific up-to-date and reliable free source for state

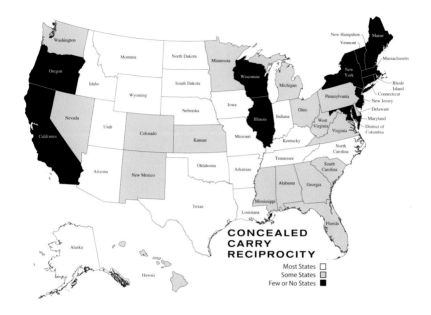

CONCEALED CARRY RECIPROCITY

Most States ☐
Some States ☐
Few or No States ■

laws and reciprocity at www.USAcarry.com.

If you are going to carry, here is what you need to know. Without a permit, traveling with a loaded and/or accessible weapon is really asking for trouble. Even though you may be 100 percent legal in some jurisdictions, it can easily depend on how a law enforcement officer interprets the law or perceives his or her safety in your presence. You could be totally in the right but find yourself detained anyway—a bummer end to what could have been a terrific road trip.

The best advice is that you do not carry a firearm on your bike without a permit. Even with a permit, do not carry a firearm out of state without doing your research through one or both of the abovementioned sources. And even if you do follow all the rules and know all the state laws, you should still expect that in a tense situation like a traffic stop, adding a loaded weapon into the equation ups the ante significantly.

> **LEGAL BRIEFS: Without a permit, traveling with a loaded and/or accessible weapon is really asking for trouble.**

2

U.S. Motorcycle Laws and Regulations

OVERVIEW

If you want to adopt a riding policy that will keep you squeaky clean no matter what state you're in, this is the chapter for you. The State-by-State Guide parses out states by their individual idiosyncrasies (idiocracies is a better term—thank you, Jay Moorehead). But if you don't want to have to worry in some faraway state whether you're legal or not, you have to get your bike, gear, and riding aligned with the U.S. baseline. This is specific guidance for what's generally legally allowed and what is not generally legally allowed in the United States. Here we summarize the laws of all 50 states, assume you're willing to conform to every last one of them to ensure a smooth trip, and dole them out as marching orders. No guarantees, of course, but if you've got all these covered, the only way you're going to get pulled over is for doing something really, really stupid.

LICENSE

In this book, I make the assumption that you have a valid driver's license with a motorcycle endorsement. If you don't have that at the very least, I cannot help you. You've got no ground to stand on. Every time you're stopped by law enforcement, you're going to end up getting your bike towed.

However, some of us are still learning and riding on motorcycle permits and don't yet have licenses. There are a few things you need to know. Scroll a little further down and you'll find the information you're looking for under "permit restrictions."

HELMET LAWS

Universal ■
Partial ☐
None ☐

HELMET LAWS

Here's the big issue: In what states am I required to wear a helmet, and in what states is it optional? If you want to be legal in every state, wear a DOT-labeled, properly fastened helmet.

Helmet laws are all over the place in this country. Most every state, except those holdouts in Illinois, Iowa, and New Hampshire, have some kind of helmet law. (Actually, scratch that—New Hampshire now has a partial helmet law.) Twenty states and Washington, D.C., have mandatory, universal helmet laws. The remaining states have modified or partial helmet laws, which usually apply to a rider based on his or her age and license status.

Statute language and enforcement vary widely. Some states where helmets are mandatory have laws written in such a way that they're relatively meaningless and unenforceable. For example, when the penalty for not wearing a helmet is a $20 fine and no points, not only are riders less vigilant about helmet compliance, but law enforcement is less interested in writing these tickets—and prosecuting them. However, a flagrant helmet violation, such as wearing a novelty helmet or no helmet, is a valid reason to initiate a traffic stop. That, of course, opens the door to all sorts of additional heartache if you're less than compliant in other areas of the law.

Quite a few states have beefed up their laws to specify certain certifications (U.S. Department of Transportation or Federal Motor Vehicle Safety Standard 218) and requirements for wearing a helmet, such as making sure the helmet is securely fastened to your head. So the advice here is that if you're going to wear a helmet, do it right by wearing a DOT-approved helmet and keeping it buckled to your head. If you're going to flaunt the law, make certain you've got a proper license, a good driving record, and current insurance with proof of it in your pocket—and that you're not riding around with beer on your breath.

FMVSS 218

The Code of Federal Regulations (CFR) lays out the minimum performance requirements for motorcycle helmets, which most states have adopted, in Title 49, Part 571, Standard Number 218. The standard defines the following:

- **the position of the helmet on the rider's head**
- **impact attenuation (reduction)**
- **helmet retention (chinstrap)**
- **labeling inside and out**
- **the testing procedure**

DOT-approved helmets with a headform inside are dropped on a flat steel anvil four times from 5 or 6 feet to test impact attenuation. The same helmet is struck twice by a pointed, 6-pound wedge to test penetration resistance. Helmets are held rigid, and the chinstraps are affixed to a machine that tests their strength by simulating loads of 50 and 300 pounds.

There's nothing you can do to test or change the characteristics of a helmet to determine if it conforms to the standard except to verify that it's labeled correctly. Proper labeling should include things like these:

- **manufacturer name**
- **model name or number and size**
- **month and year produced**
- **"DOT" symbol on the outside**
- **shell and liner construction material**
- **warnings about use and damage**

To comply with a state law that requires helmets to meet FMVSS 218 standards, you have to wear a legitimate helmet purchased from a reputable source that comes with the labeling inside and out already affixed and permanent. While most police officers are not intimate with the 218 standard, others (North Carolina comes to mind) have been well trained to identify a compliant helmet's key features—liner thickness (1 inch) and labeling being the easiest. If you're running a noncompliant helmet (as a fashion or political statement), expect that if you get stopped, you won't be moving again until you get a compliant helmet.

HELMET REFLECTORIZATION

To be safe, place a few retroreflective stickers on your helmet. A few states require reflectorization. It is uncommon, but not unheard of, for a rider to get a helmet compliance citation because he or she had no reflective material on the lid. More often, riders get dinged when getting their bikes inspected: If you show up with a helmet without reflectors in a state that requires them, they won't pass your bike until you show up with one that has them.

When helmet reflectorization is also required, it's typically a minimum of 4 square inches of reflectorized material on both sides of the helmet, if the helmet itself is not reflectorized. It is ironic that the standard warning label for helmet care advises us to not put any sort of stickers on the helmet.

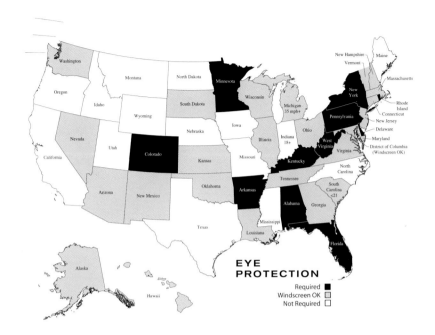

EYE PROTECTION

Required ■
Windscreen OK ▨
Not Required ☐

EYE PROTECTION

If you're trying to lay low, have something over your eyes at all times: face shield, glasses, sunglasses, or goggles. Many states accept a windshield or windscreen, but many do not; those that do may require it to be a certain height. For safety's sake, the one thing you do not want to compromise while riding is your vision. Find something you like for riding and wear it. Keep a spare handy.

PERMIT RESTRICTIONS

You'll never get pulled over for violating a permit restriction unless the cop is your angry brother-in-law (or ex-wife). But if you do get pulled over by mistake, or get tangled up in a checkpoint, you'd best be clear in demonstrating that you're complying with the laws for permit holders—not only in the state you're in, but in your home state.

Just about every state that issues a temporary learner's permit for motorcycles places some restrictions on where and when that individual can ride. The goal is to decrease a new rider's exposure to high-risk riding environments. Generally, if you're

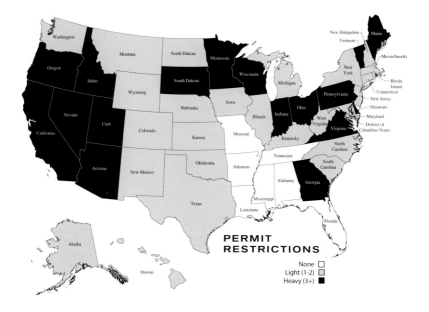

PERMIT
RESTRICTIONS

None ☐
Light (1-2) ☐
Heavy (3+) ■

riding on a motorcycle permit, you are required to obey the permit restrictions in place in the state you're riding in, not your home state. In rare cases, you're required to follow both the restrictions of your current state and your home state.

Here are some typical permit restrictions:

- **helmet required—regardless of your age**
- **no passengers**
- **no nighttime riding—half an hour after sunset until a half hour before sunrise**
- **no freeway riding—generally meaning a controlled-access, multi-lane highway**
- **adult supervision—must be in the presence of a licensed adult motorcyclist**

The best advice, if you're traveling in other states on a motorcycle permit, is to continue to follow the permit restrictions of your home state as well as the restrictions of the state you're visiting.

INSURANCE

Carrying liability insurance is mostly ubiquitous nowadays, as 99.9 percent of everywhere requires every vehicle to have it and for every driver or owner to carry proof of it. To be covered no matter where you go, and to be covered with the minimum in every state, your insurance should be at least $50,000 individual bodily injury, $100,000 aggregate or all-persons bodily injury, and $25,000 property damage. Many states' minimums are well below these numbers; these represent the maximum, and you'll find these requirements in Alaska and Maine.

The minimum basic liability coverage for bodily injury (each person involved), aggregate bodily injury (the sum of all persons involved), and property damage (the aggregate of the stuff that gets wrecked when you crash into somebody) varies widely from state to state. But what don't vary widely are states' reactions when you're caught without insurance: Expect to get your license suspended. State licensing authorities take this very seriously, because liability insurance helps protect victims when someone makes a mistake on the road.

Laws vary, but accidents that entail property damage often must be reported to the state. Some states require this for as little as $250. Also note that if you are involved in a crash, you are generally required by law to remain at the scene and "render aid" (at the very least, contact emergency personnel) for any injured person. Failing to do so can even be a felony. At the least, it is often associated with severe penalties (big points, suspensions, etc.).

Every state except Washington requires liability insurance, though the minimum amount varies. Many states also require personal injury protection (PIP), underinsured driver protection, and uninsured driver protection—though these are not always required for motorcycle riders. Most states also require that you carry proof of insurance.

ADMINISTRATIVE SANCTIONS AND SUSPENSIONS

The Oklahoma Driver's Manual sums up states' attitudes toward driver licensing and moving violations pretty succinctly: "You do not own your license. It is the property of the State . . . and can be denied, canceled, suspended, or revoked if you do not abide by the laws of the State. . . . Driving is a privilege you have earned by passing the tests and paying the application fees. Your driver's license is your legal permission to drive a car or motorcycle on the streets and highways. . . ."

Without analyzing the above paragraph too much or getting too cheeky, it should suffice to say that when dealing with license sanctions after receiving a traffic ticket, state officials consider your driver's license a gift and think you should treat it as such. Not that anyone outside of state service agrees with that, but it should help you keep things in perspective when trying to solve problems.

Every state licensing authority has some system in place to monitor driver behavior and curb it when it gets out of hand. Or put another way: They wouldn't give it to you if they couldn't take it away from you. States measure driving behavior primarily through the accumulation of traffic violations, citations, and convictions, though they also use license

LEGAL BRIEFS: Every state licensing authority has some system in place to monitor driver behavior and curb it when it gets out of hand.

Practicing stunts on a public roadway is never a good idea.

sanctions such as suspension to curb such nondriving behaviors as no insurance, failure to pay child support, or failure to pay parking tickets.

There are two general types of administrative sanctioning processes, the most commonly known system being a "demerit points" system, applied in more than half the states. The remaining states have a less calculating but equally formal system that weighs the number and type of violations by category against an arbitrary time period: two years, give or take a year. They both do the same thing (measure your behavior), and they both work about the same way: When you rack up X number of traffic violations, you have your license suspended for Y number of days—in addition to all the fines you might pay as well.

A demerit points system attaches numeric values to traffic violation convictions and sets threshold levels for when a warning letter, possible suspension, mandatory suspension, license revocation, etc., is incurred. For example, in the fictitious state of Motorcyclia, points for speed-related offenses are ascribed as follows:

Speeding 1–9 mph over	0 points (remember, this is fictitious!)
Speeding 10–14 mph over	1 point (typical transgression)
Speeding 15–24 mph over	3 points (willful flaunting of the law)
Speeding 25+ over	6 points (you should limit your riding to racetracks)
Reckless driving	5 points (innocent or intentional)

Demerit points stemming from a conviction remain on your driving record for two years in Motorcyclia. If you accumulate five points, the DMV will send you a warning letter stating that your privilege to drive is at risk. When you reach six points, the DMV will suspend your license for 30 days. After your suspension period, every time you surpass the six-point limit, your license will be suspended for 30 days for every point above six on your record. Note that penalties are generally harsher when you hold a commercial driver's license, whether or not you're driving a commercial vehicle. Underage drivers (15 to 20) and those holding provisional licenses under a graduated licensing program start getting suspended much earlier and much easier—it rarely takes more than two citations to halt the process.

Oftentimes, drivers can elect (or be required) to participate in a state-approved driver improvement clinic. This is an in-person or online education course intended to educate problem drivers about the rules of the road, risks of bad decision making, and proper behaviors expected of licensed drivers in the state. Habitual violators or those with particularly egregious offenses (such as fleeing a police officer, speeding and causing an injury or death, DWI, etc.) are likely required to take a driver improvement clinic in order to fulfill court requirements and/or get their license back. Some states allow you to take a course in lieu of adding the points to your record or to have the number of points due to a conviction lessened. You can even take a course to lower your current points to help keep you out of the red zone, or to accrue "good driving points" preemptively that can be used to fend off points received for a traffic conviction.

The other type of violation-monitoring process doesn't use points; instead, it compares the number and category or severity of traffic offenses within a certain time period. In Motorcyclia's neighbor state of Bikesylvania, license sanctions for moving violations occur as follows:

Three convictions within a two-year period	Warning letter
Four convictions within a two-year period	30-day suspension
Five convictions within a three-year period	60-day suspension
Six convictions within a four-year period	90-day suspension

In both points and nonpoints systems, many states have created laws that provide exceptions to the typical process when the violations are out of the ordinary. For example, speeding in excess of 25 to 30 mph over the limit can get your license suspended immediately, even though it may not put your driving record past the points threshold. The magic 100-mph mark (the groundspeed equivalent of breaking the sound barrier) has begun to pop up here and there, with undoubtedly more to come: "Busting the ton" has the potential to get your license immediately suspended or revoked for six months to a year.

Many states that use demerit points systems also monitor the number of convictions in a certain time period. So even if your point totals are below the high-tide mark, you can still get suspended for being a frequent flier.

Revocations are a little different from suspensions. Suspensions typically have a specific start and end date. When the suspension period ends, a driver only needs to pay the reapplication and reinstatement fees to restore driving privileges. A revocation is more indefinite. There will generally be a minimum period of time, one to three years, that has to elapse before an individual is eligible again for a license. Drivers must then also go through an investigative process to determine eligibility before being allowed to reapply, retest, and reinstate their license. Most

states have laws that require drivers who have three reckless driving convictions in a year to be revoked or suspended.

TRAFFIC VIOLATION AND ADMINISTRATIVE FINES, FEES, SURCHARGES, AND GRATUITIES

The problem with violations such as speeding tickets isn't just that the state can take away your license, it's the costs involved. The relatively minor traffic citation cost pales in comparison to the added fees that the city, county, and state place on you because you've got your wallet open. Some states don't hit you too badly when you make a minor mistake and get nabbed for 5 mph over the speed limit. But with the volume of high-speed traffic and the national agenda to reduce highway fatalities in full swing, penalties for a simple speeding ticket run in the $100 to $200 range. Big speeding tickets, where you're heading up toward the magic 100 number, are going to cost you anywhere from $250 to $500. But the reality is that these costs are minimal compared to what your insurance company will do to you when they find out.

The mathematicians who work in the insurance industry have noticed that increased liability claims are closely associated with drivers who have a problem following the rules. Therefore, insurance companies routinely monitor your driving record and jack up your rates when you start falling into the "high-risk" category. Rate increases can last for years and cost you thousands of dollars in additional premiums. Therefore, and we'll discuss this in more detail later, it is wise not to let points or citations accumulate on your driving record.

LEGAL BRIEFS: The mathematicians who work in the insurance industry have noticed that increased liability claims are closely associated with drivers who have a problem following the rules.

STATE RECIPROCITY

Reciprocity is a tricky thing. You should assume that violations in other states will be reported back to your state. Over the years, states have entered into agreements with one another to share information and keep traffic stops predictable. There are two types of interstate compacts: the Nonresident Violator Compact and the Driver License Compact. Member states of these compacts (most every state participates) cooperate with regard to driving offenses: They notify the home state of an out-of-town rider's traffic conviction for possible license suspension. Home states that conform to these compacts will also take action against you, usually in the form of an administrative suspension, if you haven't conformed to the requirements of a conviction in another state. The only benefit to drivers is that after a citation for a moving violation, the driver can be released by authorities and is not necessarily required to make a court appearance or post bond.

The Nonresident Violator Compact (NRVC) is meant to ensure equal treatment of nonresidents and residents within a state. It also is intended to standardize methods for processing citations and a driver's failure to appear or comply with the terms of a moving violation citation. This means that if you're nabbed for speeding out of your home state and you're in an NRVC state, the arresting officer can release you without posting bond for the fine. But, if you later fail to pay the fine or appear in court, your home state will suspend your license until you comply with the citation's requirements (pay the fine). States that are not members of this compact are Alaska, California, Michigan, Montana, Oregon, and Wisconsin.

The Driver License Compact is related but slightly different than the NRVC. The purpose of the compact is to assist states in administering the "one license, one driving record" concept. The only states remaining that don't adhere to the concept are Georgia, Massachusetts, Michigan, Tennessee, and Wisconsin. This doesn't mean that your home state won't find out about the ticket you received in one of these states, but it does mean you have a better chance of slipping by.

HANDLEBAR HEIGHT

No ☐
Yes ☐

RADAR DETECTORS

About 20 states forbid the use of radar detectors in commercial vehicles. But the use of radar detectors in passenger vehicles and on motorcycles is legal in every state except Oklahoma, Virginia, and the District of Columbia. However, displaying a radar detector in plain sight can often be interpreted by law enforcement as a speeding tool, and your chances of getting a speeding ticket may increase simply because it's there. If you're trying to stay below the radar, don't run one.

HANDLEBAR HEIGHT RESTRICTIONS

For some reason, lawmakers once had a very keen interest in the height of motorcyclists' handlebars. A bunch of laws were passed, long ago, and then

everybody forgot about it . . . except law enforcement and motorcyclists. Little by little, these laws are being repealed, but there are still a lot of them out there and it's an easy way to get noticed by law enforcement. You should know that in the strictest of states, bars may rise to no more than 15 inches above the operator's seat. If it's anything near or higher than that, you'll start running into problems in some states.

DAYTIME HEADLIGHT USE

If you want to avoid notice, ride with your headlight on at all times. This is not an issue for 99 percent of us, but occasionally an older, custom, or fabricated bike has an on/off switch. About half of the states require motorcycles to run the headlight all the time. I should add that the reason behind the law—rider visibility in the sea of traffic—is a valid one. There is no good reason to ride with your headlight off during the daytime except maybe a weak alternator, but that's no excuse, either: Fix your alternator!

HEADLIGHT AND TAILLIGHT MODULATORS

Often confusing but rarely a true legal issue, headlight modulators are legitimate pieces of equipment on motorcycles—and legal by national standards. Language was added to the Federal Motor Vehicle Safety Standards (FMVSS Title 49, Part 571.108) as an exception to laws that prohibit "flashing" lights on anything but an emergency vehicle. Because a properly designed headlight modulator does not flash on and off, but pulses high and low, it is legal and does the same thing you could do with your left thumb if you wanted. There are specifications regarding the intensity and rate at which the headlight pulses, as well as requirements that it only operate during daylight hours.

Law enforcement officers often do not know or understand the legality of headlight modulators, so many riders have gotten tickets for using them that they've had to fight in court. Cops see something that looks like a flashing light, understand that they're the only ones who are supposed to have flashing lights, stop you, and write you a ticket. If you're going to use a headlight modulator, expect to get hassled about it from time to time.

DAYTIME HEADLIGHT USE

Not Required ☐
Required ☐

Ironically, the same standards that make headlight modulators legal do not go so far as to make taillight modulators legal. Like a headlight modulator, you could mimic a taillight modulator by pumping the brakes when you stop (and many of us do). But a device that does so and allows us to devote full attention to slowing safely is generally not legal because it seems to fall into the category of flashing lights. It is interesting to note that due to the combination and proximity of taillight and stop lamp, in practice these devices often do pulse the light high and low, but no matter. Fortunately, it is nearly unheard of that a rider receives a ticket for using a taillight modulator.

LEFT LANE RESTRICTION

Several states have laws that reserve the left lane on a multi-lane road for passing only (hooray for those states!). The scope and spirit of the laws vary so widely that they're hard to quantify, so the best approach is to view the left lane philosophically. Stay out of it unless you're passing someone.

Regardless of whether there's a law, nothing infuriates otherwise conscientious drivers more than someone who drives slowly in the left lane for no apparent reason. And if you're going to use the left lane to pass, don't dawdle—get it over with and get back over to the right. Holding up traffic because you've got the cruise control set just where you like it is just as infuriating. Even if you plan to pass every single car on the road, you still need to move back to the right after every pass.

LEGAL BRIEFS: **Regardless of whether there's a law, nothing infuriates otherwise conscientious drivers more than someone who drives slowly in the left lane for no apparent reason.**

UNCHANGING TRAFFIC SIGNAL LAWS (OR RED LIGHT LAWS)

A handful of states—eleven, at last count—have devised legislative solutions to the problem of motorcyclists sitting at a red light indefinitely because their bikes went undetected by the sensors. Many states' traffic codes require the sensors to be calibrated to detect smaller vehicles such as motorcycles and bicycles. Other laws explicitly permit riders to use their best judgment and proceed through the red light if it won't change. Still others are "affirmative defenses," meaning you can get a citation for disobeying a stoplight, but if you can prove in court that you followed the correct procedures for doing so, you can have the ticket dismissed. These laws are few and far between, however (though becoming more common), so for the sake of staying below the radar, do not attempt to blow off a red light in the presence of a law enforcement officer. Take a right and then a U-turn. Or wait for a car to pull up behind you.

But if you're the independent sort who believes you can make your own decisions regarding your own and other drivers' safety, there are "rules" for how to proceed or turn on an unchanging red light. They are more or less variations of the following:

- **You have come to a complete stop.**
- **The light does not recognize your motorcycle or the light is not working properly.**

UNCHANGING TRAFFIC SIGNAL LAW

Yes ☐
No ☑

- **You have waited an inordinately long time, meaning three minutes or one or more full stoplight cycles.**
- **There is no traffic approaching or you can proceed or turn without creating a safety hazard.**

Most states have language that deals with "nonfunctioning" signal lights. The procedure at that point is to treat the signal like a four-way stop. It could be argued that an unchanging signal is a nonfunctioning signal and should be treated as such. Again, doing this right in front of the law is just begging for a stop. But if you've got a silver tongue and enjoy fighting traffic citations in court, you may have an angle to use.

LEGAL BRIEFS: A handful of states—eleven, at last count—have devised legislative solutions to the problem of motorcyclists sitting at a red light indefinitely because their bikes went undetected by the sensors.

TURN SIGNALS

States are about half and half as far as requiring electric turn signals mounted on the motorcycle. Regardless of whether you have to have them or not, most states require you to signal your turns and lane changes no matter what, meaning by use of hand signals if you don't have electric signals. Some states go so far as to put requirements on signaling that include visible distances, day or night—so in some cases you could conceivably be cited for not using a signal, even if you did, because from 100 feet behind you the cop could not see your signal clearly.

So, always signal your turns and lane changes at least 100 feet in advance, and be cognizant that riding after dark might put you at risk. If you don't have turn signals or they don't work, you're quite often required by law to use these signals: left arm straight out for a left turn, left arm cocked upward at 90 degrees for a right, and left arm cocked 90 degrees downward for slowing or stopping. Obviously, you use your left hand to avoid losing control over the throttle.

TURN
SIGNALS

Not Required ☐
Required Except for Older Bikes ☐
Required for All Bikes ■

LICENSE PLATE DISPLAY

Some states haven't gotten around to it yet; others have packed their law books to the gills with requirements for how a license plate is supposed to be mounted. It seems like a simple piece of metal to many of us, but law enforcement officials take it very, very seriously. Think about it philosophically: Officers rely heavily on license plates as a reliable way to identify a vehicle's owner at a glance. (Of course, just glancing at your plate won't identify you, but there is the assurance that if the need arises to know who owns that vehicle, they can find out.) For example, if you're a pedestrian in a crosswalk and an SUV runs you down and then drives away—and someone got the plate number—this means that the person who broke the law and put you in the hospital has a better chance of being held accountable for their actions.

To be covered in every state, your plate should be mounted just under the taillight, with a white light illuminating it and making it readable at night from 50 feet. It should be mounted in a rigid (fixed) position so it doesn't swing, and the

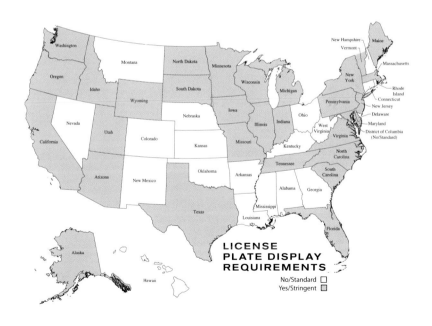

LICENSE PLATE DISPLAY REQUIREMENTS

No/Standard ☐
Yes/Stringent ◼

bottom edge of the plate should be horizontal to the ground. The plate should also face straight back from the motorcycle—not slightly up, not slightly down. There should be no license plate frame, decorations, or any kind of a cover on it, even a clear one. Your goal with your license plate position and orientation is that you are proudly displaying your identity for all the world to see, and you'd never, ever want to hide any part of the plate from anyone trying to read it.

In the State-by-State Guide, each state-at-a-glance will have an entry for license plate display. If it says "no," that means that license plates are just supposed to point backward and be plainly visible; there aren't a lot of specific rules you have to follow. If it says "yes," there are finer points you should know about your plate before you travel in that state.

FENDERS

You should have two fenders on your bike, front and rear, to be covered in every state. Many muddy, sandy, and rocky states have laws that require vehicles to have fenders to protect other vehicles from all the stuff your tires spit backwards. I suspect that years ago, before asphalt was so ubiquitous, muddy, dusty gravel roads were problematic if you weren't the first vehicle in line. (This is why bikes new from the showroom come with sometimes ungodly and ungainly awful plastic shrouds that stick way out behind the bike . . . and which are usually promptly removed or modified by riders. See also: "Reflectors.") About half of the states require at least one fender, and most require both fenders.

EXHAUST NOISE

State exhaust noise laws are rarely aimed directly at motorcyclists. The laws for running a muffler that remains in "constant operation," do not allow the vehicle to emit any "excessive or unusual noise," and is not modified in any way ("cutouts, bypasses") to make it louder than stock apply to every vehicle on the road (cars, trucks, and motorcycles). The laws sometimes make exceptions for exceptional vehicles, such as big rigs and nonstandard road users. These laws

LEGAL BRIEFS: You should have two fenders on your bike, front and rear, to be covered in every state.

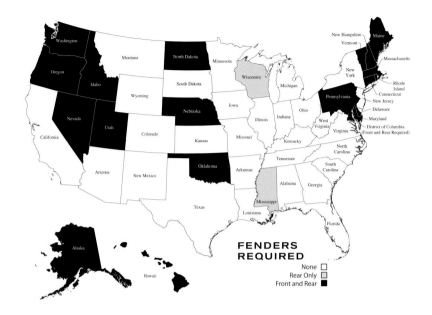

Washington
Montana
North Dakota
Minnesota
New Hampshire
Vermont
Maine
Oregon
Idaho
South Dakota
Wisconsin
Michigan
New York
Massachusetts
Rhode Island
Connecticut
Wyoming
Pennsylvania
New Jersey
Nevada
Utah
Colorado
Nebraska
Iowa
Illinois
Indiana
Ohio
West Virginia
Virginia
Delaware
Maryland
District of Columbia (Front and Rear Required)
California
Kansas
Missouri
Kentucky
North Carolina
Arizona
New Mexico
Oklahoma
Arkansas
Tennessee
South Carolina
Texas
Mississippi
Alabama
Georgia
Louisiana
Florida
Alaska
Hawaii

FENDERS REQUIRED

None ☐
Rear Only ☐
Front and Rear ■

refer to the Environmental Protection Agency standard (40 CFR, Ch. 1, Part 205, D/E), which limits motorcycle noise levels to about 80 decibels, whether stock or aftermarket. The regulation also includes labeling requirements that state that the pipe is compliant with the EPA standard. Many states, it should be noted, do not require the EPA standard and set their own limit from 80 to 100 decibels or so. Obviously, the safest bet is to run a stock pipe. Even running an aftermarket pipe that is claimed to be *quieter* than stock (yeah, right) could be risky.

Local ordinances and attitudes, too many to count, are a much greater concern when it comes to noise. Citizens in areas that are popular among motorcyclists have grown more and more vocal about excessive motorcycle noise over the years, and the local police departments are listening. (The perception among many citizens, however, is that they're not listening.) The fact is, many of the best places to ride are also the best places to live, for the same reasons: natural beauty, low traffic volume, and peace and quiet. Many communities try to ban motorcycles from certain areas outright, but few succeed.

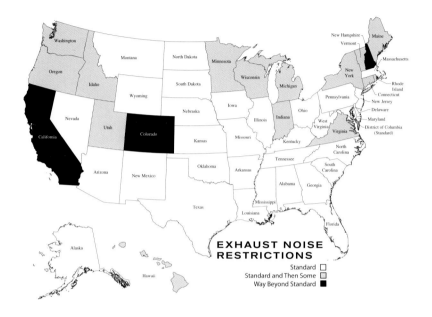

EXHAUST NOISE RESTRICTIONS

Standard ☐
Standard and Then Some ☐
Way Beyond Standard ■

More commonly, law enforcement officers are quick to act when they perceive a motorcycle exhaust to be too loud. They often will issue a ticket that is unrelated to exhaust noise laws, such as disturbing the peace, public nuisance, engine braking, etc. As noise levels are difficult to measure and equally difficult to enforce, you have to be running a pretty ugly pipe to get nicked for a noncompliant exhaust. But as an excuse for pulling over a motorcyclist to see what else might be found, they don't come much easier.

LEGAL BRIEFS: Citizens in areas that are popular among motorcyclists have grown more and more vocal about excessive motorcycle noise over the years, and the local police departments are listening.

Even so, a fair number of local communities have succeeded in tamping down motorcycle noise, at least temporarily, usually by encouraging law enforcement to check for EPA stamps and issue citations (as in Albuquerque; New York City; Arvada, Colorado; Portland, Maine; and Green Bay, Wisconsin). However, the city of Denver is the most well known; it effectively requires all bikes to have stock equipment only. The city of Boston levies huge ($300) fines for riders running illegal pipes. And the state of California has recently put some pretty strict measures in place.

A few places around the United States are noted for being particularly strict with motorcycle exhausts. But for the most part, a pipe that does what it's supposed to do (that is, muffle sound) skips by under the radar. In practice, the place you'll run into the most trouble for a modified and/or overloud exhaust is during your state's vehicle inspection process, if you have one.

If you're running unbaffled or straight pipes, or have a particularly repetitive revving hand, you should expect to draw attention in smaller communities, especially those that are relatively touristy. Fortunately, even with an overly loud pipe, much of the sound emitted has more to do with the rider's behavior than the exhaust system itself—and cops know this. If you are polite, avoid marking your territory with sound, and stay easy on the throttle in town, you shouldn't have too many problems. An interesting—if irrelevant—sidelight is that loud pipes don't necessarily lead to increased engine power, and they often reduce power by reducing exhaust-gas scavenging. This is particularly true with an otherwise stock engine.

In the State-by-State Guide, each state-at-a-glance will have an entry for exhaust noise. If it says "no," that means that your exhaust should be in good working condition and not use any sort of cutout or bypass that makes it louder. There aren't a lot of other specific rules you have to follow. If it says "yes," there are finer points you should know about your pipe before you travel in that state, and those are listed later.

EARPHONES

Probably not on the forefront of most motorcyclists' minds, but something to be aware of, is the 15 or so states that have something to say about using earphones or headphones. To be fair, these laws apply to all drivers. To be compliant in every state, don't use them while riding. However, there are lots of exceptions worth noting, which are all included in the State-by-State Guide. For example, helmet speakers are always okay. What we're talking about with the earphones are the

EARPHONES

Permitted ☐
One Ear Only ☐
Not Permitted ■

little headsets or inserts that come with music players that cover or plug your ears and block just about every sound except what you want to hear. Earphones used for communication (a bike-to-bike intercom, hands-free cell phone, or CB radio) are often okay, but those used for entertainment (XM or iPod) are not. Some states allow a rider to use an earphone in one ear only.

CHECKPOINTS

Sobriety checkpoints are popping up all over the country, and some states' practices have begun to show characteristics of being motorcycle-specific. Drinking and driving is seen as a pandemic in this country, and federal and state governments are obligated to find solutions. One solution is establishing a highway checkpoint, where cars, trucks, and motorcycles are pulled aside, usually randomly, to see if the driver is impaired by alcohol or drugs. About four-

CHECKPOINTS

No ☐
Yes ☐

fifths of states use checkpoints as
an enforcement tool. A dozen states do
not, usually based on constitutional and
legal obstacles.

Checkpoints are rarely "sneaky" tactics;
quite the opposite. The agencies conducting
the checkpoints announce ahead of time that
they're going to be doing it, and where, because the goal is not as much to
arrest drunk drivers as it is to deter impaired driving. A few agencies across
the country prefer the element of surprise when it comes to checkpoints and
enforcement saturations, but the going strategy is to make sure drivers know
it's going to happen so they can make better decisions before getting behind
the wheel (or throwing a leg over). I am dead serious when I tell you that a
checkpoint that nets not a single drunk driver is considered a success in
most states. If you haven't been drinking, checkpoints are generally no more
than an inconvenience.

AUTOMATED ENFORCEMENT

Technology in the form of red light cameras and speed cameras have opened the door to automated enforcement, and about half of states use these tools, primarily in heavily populated areas. Most photographic enforcement is focused on drivers who run red lights or exceed the speed limit, though there are a fair number of instances of cameras that monitor railroad crossings and toll booths. Speeding cameras can be hard mounted on some stationary object, or they can be mobile and operate out of a van. On some toll roads, drivers are timed between stops and can be issued a citation for making record time.

> **LEGAL BRIEFS:** Automated enforcement often doesn't carry the same weight as a bona fide traffic stop with a police officer as a witness. Due to the difficulty of prosecuting this type of citation, penalties are often lower and the citation is left off the driving record.

Automated enforcement often doesn't carry the same weight as a bona fide traffic stop with a police officer as a witness. The person who receives the ticket

AUTOMATED ENFORCEMENT

No ☐
Yes ☐

is usually the registered owner of the vehicle. Due to the difficulty of prosecuting this type of citation, penalties are often lower and the citation is left off the driving record. This makes it easier for folks to buckle and just send in the money, rather than fight.

SCHOOL BUSES

There's not a single state in the United States that doesn't require you to stop for a school bus when it is loading or unloading children. And the worried parents of the world thank you for being patient at the handlelbars while our kids are finding their own way to and from school. The details of when, where, and how you stop for a school bus vary slightly from state to state, but the effect is the same: When the red lights are flashing, you stop. Most states do not require you to stop on multi-lane divided roadways when you're approaching from the opposite direction, but a few (including Arkansas, Mississippi, New York, and West Virginia) do.

The best approach, to be legal in every state, is to begin to slow and prepare to stop when you see a bus with flashing amber lights. When the lights go red, or when the stop arm at the driver's window comes out, or both, you stop at least 25 feet from the bus. Do not proceed until A) the stop arm is retracted and the red lights stop flashing, B) the bus resumes motion, or C) the driver waves you by. Bus drivers can catch your license plate as you pass illegally and report you to the local constabulary as many as 24 hours after the fact.

PEDESTRIANS

Laws requiring vehicles to yield to pedestrians vary slightly, but the message is the same: Pedestrians have the right of way at intersections, and you're required to let them cross safely. The reality is, pedestrians were here first (120+ years ago), and this land is their land, not our land. Pedestrians are equally liable to obey

the laws and cross only where and when it's allowed, but the lives and limbs at stake still give pedestrians the priority.

Most states specify that you yield to a pedestrian in a crosswalk—or one who is about to enter a crosswalk, marked or unmarked. Oftentimes, this means that you stop until the pedestrian no longer occupies your half of the road. Entering a road from an alley or driveway, you generally have to yield to any pedestrian, anywhere. The laws also usually include language that says it's illegal to pass any vehicle that is stopped for a pedestrian. This makes sense, as there could be something the other driver sees but you don't. And this can cause you trouble, because many well-meaning drivers will stop if there's a pedestrian, or bicyclist, anywhere near the crosswalk.

Most states have special rules regarding blind pedestrians, as evidenced by the white cane or canine assistant. You pretty much have to stop or yield to these folks no matter where they are; otherwise, you face really big fines and sanctions from the local licensing authority.

Be aware that in practice, lots of riders and drivers have no clue that they're supposed to yield or stop. Because the active enforcement and promotion of pedestrian crossing laws is relatively new, slowing or stopping for a pedestrian should be accompanied by a vigorous flashing of your brake light to warn any vehicle that is on your tail.

PASSENGER AGE RESTRICTIONS

Forty-five states have no minimum age for passengers. Lousiana, Texas, and Washinton restrict passengers to age 5 and above, while you must be at least 7 in Hawaii and 8 in Arkansas. Many states require that all passengers are able to touch the footrests, and virtually every state requires a helmet on anyone under 18.

WORK ZONES

Every state has laws that increase fines and penalties when you commit a moving violation in a highway work zone. Fines are usually doubled, and second or third offenses get downright expensive (and the "hotel" you get to stay in isn't the greatest). About half of the states only apply these increased penalties if workers are actually present in the work zone. See www.ghsa.org for the most current breakdown of work zone laws.

MOVE-OVER LAWS

When your job involves working at the roadside on the highway, you're at risk every moment you're within a car's width of the fog line. Highway workers, utility workers, highway helpers, and law enforcement officers are struck and killed all the time when working on the shoulder. Almost every state has enacted a "move over" law requiring drivers, when coming up upon an emergency vehicle with its lights flashing, to vacate the lane closest to the emergency vehicle and change

EXCESSIVE SPEED SANCTIONS

No ☐
Yes ☑

lanes. When doing so is not possible or advisable, drivers are required to slow down until they're past the vehicle. States have been known to conduct "move over" enforcement to raise awareness of the laws, which are relatively new in most states.

The advice to motorcycle riders here is keep your head and eyes up on the horizon. Give yourself plenty of time to see the flashing lights and find a safe place to move over. And if you can't, roll off the throttle and move to the leftmost portion of the lane. It wouldn't hurt to give the worker or police officer a little nod or a wave to let them know you understand the law and are paying attention.

EXCESSIVE SPEED SANCTIONS

A few states have become fed up with the mayhem caused by excessive speed, whether real or imagined (the mayhem, not the speed), and have enacted positively draconian fines and consequences for driving at a rate that is significantly higher than the norm. Not all states do it—and on that note, not many states do it—but states are moving in that direction. The magic number seems to be 100 mph. (Would it be 120 mph if humans had six fingers and toes instead of five?) You should also assume, as many states do, that speeding drivers forfeit their right of way in an intersection or merge area.

MANDATORY TOW

Few and far between, some states require that if you're caught driving without a proper license (or license endorsement!), your vehicle is taken away from you. Most of the time, the decision is up to the discretion of the law enforcement officer. And in my experience, they only tow you if they absolutely have to (99 percent of the time) or if they're bent on being a complete and utter jerk (1 percent). However, this information is not important, because if you're reading this book you're way past the point in your life when you're driving around with no license.

HOV LANES

High-occupancy vehicle (HOV) lanes, which we used to call carpool lanes, are meant to be open to motorcycles. However, states can override this if local conditions make it such that it becomes a safety problem. Most often, there will be a sign or traffic-control device that specifically prohibits motorcycles from using the HOV lane at that time. In the State-by-State Guide, each state's approach to HOV lanes, if they have them, is noted. But for the sake of staying below the radar, don't worry about it—assume you can use an HOV lane

on your motorcycle unless you see a sign or variable message board (black and orange electronic sign) that specifically excludes motorcyclists.

FEET DOWN AT A STOP

At last, an urban myth. My hunch is that a nonrider imagined it must be so, and the idea caught on that it's the law. Maybe somewhere along the line, some state or municipality actually created a law that required riders to put a foot, or both feet, down at stops, but nowhere in any state statutes can any law like that be found today. Yet the belief prevails among riders and law enforcement: Not putting your feet down at a stop means you didn't come to a complete stop and you can be ticketed.

It's probably true in 99 percent of cases that when a rider does not put her foot down at a stop that she does not come to a complete stop. But these two factors are coincidental, not cause and effect. It is entirely possible to put your foot down without stopping, just as it is entirely possible—though not easy—to come to a complete stop without putting a foot down.

Like most driving behaviors, it's best not to try your luck in front of a member of the local constabulary. If there's a cop anywhere nearby, make it a point to put your foot down. But for those of you who are adept at the "instantaneous stop," in which all motion ceases and the rider is perfectly balanced and ready to take off again, you're entirely within your rights to keep your feet on your pegs. And if you want to learn this high-skill technique, it takes lots of practice and lots of trial and error. It's something that should be practiced in a parking lot—not at stop signs. The key to doing it successfully is to waste no time between stopping and going. Release the clutch immediately after stopping. Note that to the untrained eye

(most of them out there), stopping and going that quickly looks an awful lot like a rolling stop.

If you're a good enough rider that you can stop without putting your feet down, you should probably dab one down anyway, just to be polite. You should especially do so at four-way stops where folks have to take turns: It helps everybody decide who gets to go next.

ERRATICS

In geologic terms, an erratic is a rock or rock formation that differs in shape, size, and/or composition from the rock surrounding it. Typically, an erratic is transported a long way from its origin by a glacier. For our purposes, an erratic is a traffic law or motorcycle law that is relatively unique to a state or local jurisdiction.

There are a few erratics that motorcycle riders need to know about. (Denver, Colorado's OEM-exhaust-only law is the poster child for this type of law.) Mostly they involve really weird laws or really harsh consequences for a violation in one state that is mostly a non-issue in every other state.

I consider a couple other types of laws "erratics" even though they're actually pretty much universal. One is that coasting—riding along with the transmission in neutral—is not allowed, anywhere. Well, it's probably allowed some places, but nowhere that I could find. I wasn't looking for it but happened across it at least three dozen times, so it's good to know. Keep your bike in gear, especially on long downhills when you might be tempted to give your clutch hand a break because you're only going to use the brakes for the next 10 minutes anyway.

Another universal erratic is the law that says motorcycle riders can't cling to other vehicles. (This sounds like the law against putting your arm out of the school bus window, but no matter.) Apparently, back in 1940 or whenever most of these laws were passed, there must have been some terrific disaster in all the papers in which a pregnant prom queen with a milk crate full of super-cute puppies fell down and was run over while clinging to a pickup truck—probably getting some assistance from a well-meaning parishioner who knew that she'd get tired halfway to the orphanage in Boise and decided to help her along with a few extra horsepower.

ERRATICS

No ☐
Yes ☐

LANE SHARING

From a safety perspective, the advice is: don't do it. The standard for safely riding in a group of bikes is to ride in a staggered formation. But as far as protecting your driving record, side-by-side

is fine except in Vermont and Virginia, where it's illegal in both states. Riding side-by-side ("two abreast") is perfectly legal in the other 48 states.

Lane sharing with vehicles other than motorcycles or riding between lanes of traffic is not legal anywhere, including California. However, it is tolerated in California to a large degree. (See "California" in the State-by-State Guide for more information.)

VEHICLE INSPECTIONS

Many states require a physical safety inspection by a licensed state worker or contractor. Fail the inspection and you cannot get a tag for your plate to ride that year. It often doesn't matter if a component was OEM or an aftermarket add-on that you installed of your own free will—if it's mounted on the bike, it must be in working and safe operating condition. States that require inspections are noted in the State-by-State Guide. What exactly your inspection entails is another matter. Below is a general overview of what you should expect to demonstrate to the scrutineers.

Brakes: Levers, lines, calipers, and pads all have to be ready to do their job with no leaks or excessive wear. One brake front or rear capable of stopping the motorcycle in a state-specified distance at a determined speed is always required. Some states require both front and rear brakes and that a rupture in one will not cause the loss of braking ability of the other.

Chain: If your bike is equipped with one, it must fit and be adjusted properly with no kinks or binding. A chain guard will be required. If you've removed it, the inspector may reject the bike.

Exhaust: States look at exhausts, at a minimum, from this perspective: The bike should be equipped with a muffler or other noise-reducer in working order and constant operation. The muffler cannot have any sort of "cutout," "bypass," or similar modification, nor can it have any obviously shoddy repairs. Some states go further and state that the exhaust cannot be modified in any way to increase the sound above OEM levels. Many states require that an exposed exhaust also include a heat shield to prevent those awful leg burns. If you're running a pipe that doesn't have an EPA stamp on it or, worse, reads "FOR COMPETITION USE ONLY" or "FOR OFF-ROAD USE ONLY," you're probably not going to pass inspection.

Frame/Chassis: The frame and swingarm must be in sound, functional condition to serve their intended purposes. The bike can have no protruding metal, plastic, or rubber parts that are loose or pointy. Side and center stands need to be sturdy and strong enough to support the bike.

Headlight: States set minimum and maximum parameters for light intensity (brightness), position on the motorcycle (centered), and orientation (aim). Headlight systems are generally required to have a dimmer switch and high-beam indicator. All electrical switches and bulbs must work as advertised, and some states even provide specifications for the energy supply (generator, fuses, etc.)— even for the way the battery is secured in the bike.

Horn: Your horn must be in good working order and audible generally at 200 feet. States also prohibit any nonemergency vehicle from running a nonstandard warning device such as a siren, bell, or whistle, unless it's an antitheft device.

License Plate: It is generally required that you have a white light to illuminate the plate. It should be mounted securely to prevent swinging, mounted horizontally to prevent a law enforcement officer from having to cock his or her head to one side to read it, and placed so the face of the plate is at a 90-degree angle to the ground, facing directly behind the bike. Heavily modified placements, such as between the tire and subframe, twisted 90 degrees and placed at the axle, or bent around some other part of the bike are likely to get your inspection sticker withheld until you comply with the required positioning.

LEGAL BRIEFS: **It is generally required that you have a white light to illuminate the license plate.**

Mirrors: Nearly every state requires at least one rearview mirror. Many states require two or else specify on which side the single mirror is placed. Mirrors often are required to be 10 or more square inches of reflective surface and cannot be cracked, broken, or missing. The view through the mirror generally needs to be at least 200 feet.

Reflectors: Requirements vary a bit from state to state, but there is a universal minimum requirement that a bike has at least one red reflector on the rear. Some states call out the requirement for additional amber reflectors on the front and back (sides). There's a reason they come from the showroom with all those awful reflectors attached!

Seats: The operator's seat must be permanently mounted. Footrests or footpegs must be permanently mounted as well. If there's a passenger seat, there must also be passenger footpegs (and sometimes passenger handholds), and vice versa. If your bike is equipped with highway pegs, there are often requirements for how far apart they are (26 inches, for example) and how far from the brake and shift levers they are (15 inches, for example).

Speedometer and Odometer: Rarely required, these gauges must work if they're attached to the bike. Lenses must not be cracked or discolored to the point where the indicators are unreadable.

LEGAL BRIEFS: **Many states set parameters for how much or little rake and trail is allowed.**

Steering: Front end components and steering head bearings need to operate smoothly without any binding, revving, stretching cables, etc. Many states set parameters for how much or little rake and trail is allowed. Handlebars must meet state requirements for distance between the grips as well as height, and many states have laws stating that handlebars have to be sturdy and unbent. Repaired or clearly "bent-back" bars will not pass muster. Inspectors also look for handgrips that are, well, grippy and not smooth or worn or slippery.

Suspension: Each piece of your suspension, namely your front fork tubes, needs to operate safely and as advertised. No leaks, binding, or overt bouncing is permitted. If your bike has a rear shock or shocks, they need to meet the same criteria.

Taillight: A red tail lamp that is illuminated whenever the headlight is on is a requirement on every inspector's list, and the limit is generally set at two, right and left, spaced evenly apart no more than X inches and no more or less than Y inches from the ground. The taillight needs to be visible at night for several hundred feet. Each taillight will be required to have a stop lamp, actuated by the brake lever and/or pedal. Most states require a white license plate lamp.

Throttle and Fuel: The throttle grip must operate as the manufacturer intended (spring back to closed when released). The fuel system cannot have any leaks, and a gas cap must be in place.

Tires: Your road rubber must be in safe operating condition and not worn down to the threads. Tires cannot be touching or rubbing any part of the motorcycle. They must also be tires meant for the wheels they're on. Those rebels out there who insist on using car tires on their bikes might not like the results come inspection time. Inspectors may also measure your tread depth; anything less than the minimum standard of 1/16 of an inch will get your bike rejected. Wheels have to be predictably round and not in any obvious state of disrepair.

> LEGAL BRIEFS: **Rebels out there who insist on using car tires on their bikes might not like the results come inspection time.**

Turn Signals: When required, or when mounted on a motorcycle whether required or not, turn signals must be operational and blink with a specified frequency range (one to two flashes per second).

Windshield: Yes, there are even requirements for your windshield, referred to as glazing, even though windshields are not required equipment. The surface and coating of your windscreen, especially if you need to look through it to see the road, must be intact—that is, free of scratches, cracks, and marring so as to keep it clear. Any stickers applied to the windscreen must be near the bottom or the edges so that they don't block the rider's view.

GOOD RESOURCES
State Laws: http://public.findlaw.com/traffic-ticket-violation-law/state-traffic-law/
American Motorcyclist Association (State Motorcycle Laws): www.amadirectlink.com/legisltn/laws.asp
Governors Highway Safety Association: www.ghsa.org

3

Ensuring a Safe Stop

Spend any amount of time on public roads and, sooner or later, you'll get stopped by law enforcement. Your behavior during a stop can make a significant difference in whether you end up having a friendly roadside conversation, getting a warning, receiving a traffic ticket, or getting arrested.

A traffic stop can be a high-stress situation for both rider and police officer. You have limited options available to you—and you have a limited time to make decisions. The actions you choose can have effects, negative and positive, on the outcome of the stop, whether right there on the side of the highway or down the road a ways when you're fighting a speeding ticket in court.

The federal government has recently undertaken the task of developing a training module for law enforcement officers in how to conduct safe roadside stops of motorcycle riders. The project staff solicited input from motorcycle riding and law enforcement experts—including the author of this book—in the characteristics and behavior of motorcyclists and what each should expect during a traffic stop. The project authors took a close look at multiple motorcycle stop scenarios with a goal of protecting the safety of both riders and law enforcement. Much of the

LEGAL BRIEFS: Your behavior during a stop can make a significant difference in whether you end up having a friendly roadside conversation, getting a warning, receiving a traffic ticket, or getting arrested.

information in this chapter is based on discussions during the research phase of the project.

Even when this new information and training is available to the public, it will take some time for it to flow outward from Washington and find its way into the hands of the police officers who interact regularly with motorcyclists. Let this chapter be your guide in fulfilling *your* obligations as a motorist and a rider to ensure a safe roadside stop experience.

STEREOTYPES

Motorcyclist stereotypes prevail in this country primarily because most people only know what they see on TV or in the movies. Many police officers also don't know much about motorcycle riders—but because of their training and experience in traffic enforcement, they probably know more than a typical American.

Most motorists are not aware of it, but a random traffic stop can be a dangerous situation for a law enforcement officer. He or she doesn't know if they're pulling over a sociopathic drug dealer on a suicide mission or a dentist from suburbia out for a Sunday ride. They are on their guard, expecting the worst and hoping for the best. But make no mistake: They are usually ready for anything. In the back of their minds, they have to expect you either to pull a gun on them or attempt to flee. It is your responsibility to demonstrate to them that you have no intention or ability to do either one.

There are a few factors that will go into every officer's decision to hit the lights and pull you over. Obviously, if you commit a moving violation, or appear to have committed one, you're liable to get stopped—especially during special enforcement waves when cops are saturating an area and arresting drunk drivers. Any excuse to get a driver pulled over to see if they've been drinking is fair game.

LEGAL BRIEFS: **Most motorists are not aware of it, but a random traffic stop can be a dangerous situation for a law enforcement officer.**

There are also behavioral cues cops use when looking for impaired riders—any one of them could get you stopped.

The following cues claim a 50 percent or better probability of indicating an alcohol-impaired rider. Note that they could also easily indicate a new or inexperienced rider, road surface problems, gusty winds, distraction, heat exhaustion, dehydration, hypothermia, poor riding posture, poor planning, or poor decision making:

- **drifting or unsteady balance during a turn or curve**
- **having trouble dismounting the motorcycle**
- **having trouble with balance when stopped**
- **late braking during a turn**
- **having an improper lean angle during a turn**
- **making erratic movements during a turn**
- **being inattentive to your surroundings**
- **inappropriate or unusual behavior**
- **weaving within your lane**

The following cues claim a 30 to 49 percent probability of indicating an impaired rider, and can get you nicked as well:

- **making erratic movements while going straight**
- **riding (at night) without a headlight**
- **tailgating**
- **going the wrong way (on a one-way street or the wrong side of the road)**

Another consideration police officers may use when deciding to pull over a rider is geographic location. If there's no safe place to make a stop, or traffic is moving fast and heavy, a cop may wait for a better opportunity to make a stop—or a better target. A dangerous mountain road with no shoulders and plenty of sport-riding bikes and cars whizzing by doesn't leave a lot of room to stand by the side of the road next to a stopped bike and write a ticket.

What you're wearing, or not wearing, may also help an officer make a decision. A well-dressed motorcyclist with top-quality riding gear head-to-toe may be perceived as less a menace to society than one who is sporting no helmet or a novelty helmet, dreadlocks, a leather vest with full-patch gang colors, and a Crocodile Dundee–style bowie knife. A younger rider is perceived as more of a fleeing threat than an old dog with a beard. If you're wearing full leathers, gloves, and boots but no helmet, you may be demonstrating a sporting, aggressive attitude but little concern for your own safety.

Even the make, model, and condition of your motorcycle can be a factor in whether an officer decides to stop you. Take a look at your bike and riding gear and ask yourself if you're sending any unintended messages with your appearance.

GETTING PULLED OVER

Officers may follow you for awhile, or may ride alongside of you for awhile, to gather such information as your physical description, bike make and model, license plate number, and any other identifying characteristics before they stop you. They're trying to learn as much as they can so that if you decide to flee, they're not automatically obligated to give chase—they can just swing by your house later with some friends and arrest you. If you notice a police officer pacing you, that's a good time to start looking for a safe, well-lit place off the road to stop for gas . . . or a snack . . . or a movie.

An officer, spotting a potential offender on a motorcycle, has no idea with whom he or she is about to make contact. Traffic stops are the least predictable part of police work. Officers are trained to make stops with extreme caution and high situational awareness—they're on edge from the beginning. But there are several things that riders can do (or not do) that can make the situation less tense. A lone rider with an out-of-state plate in the middle of nowhere, or one traveling with a passenger, is seen as generally less of a threat than are other riders. Everyone else is a potential problem.

The severity of your traffic infraction, real or imagined, will have a bearing on the police officer's initial attitude toward you. If you just made an illegal turn

from a stop in a confusing area, the officer might be fairly relaxed and figure it's a routine stop. If you just slowed down from a buck-10 after riding a standup wheelie for a quarter mile, he or she is liable to be a little more confrontational—you're demonstrating some aggressive behavior, and it will affect the officer's attitude toward you right out of the gate. When the cop hits his lights, don't bang a downshift right away and make it look like you're preparing to run.

It is possible that the officer had a glance at your driving record before making contact with you. If you have a colorful and consistent history of moving violations or a history of fleeing law enforcement officers instead of stopping—or if the officer has even a perception of that type of history (maybe he thinks he's seen you and your bike before, and you got away)—expect to be treated a little more abruptly. If the cop suspects you're impaired due to drug or alcohol use, he is not likely to be as open-minded as he might be if you're just leaving your driveway at 8:30 A.M. on a Sunday.

Once you're stopped, there are a few additional cues that may put the police officer on alert. Shut the engine off when the cop asks you to—or better yet, shut it off before he or she asks you to. Keeping hands on handlebars may appear like you're preparing to split. It's okay to sit up, take your hands off the bars, and hold them out away from your body so the officer can see them. Don't look back at the cop like you're trying to size him up, and don't start (noticeably) scanning the area—it might imply that you're looking for an opportunity to escape. (You should, subtly, scan the area so that you're aware of your position, other traffic, witnesses, and anything else that might help you later on down the road. But keep it subtle—you don't want to alarm the cop.) Keeping one foot on the motorcycle, rather than both feet on the ground, is another unconscious indicator that you're ready to move if you have to. Don't give the officer any reason to be suspicious of you.

FINDING A SAFE PLACE TO STOP

You rarely get to choose where you stop when law enforcement decides to pull you over. Most police officers will attempt to pick a safe spot where visibility

is good and there's plenty of room at the roadside—he or she doesn't want to get run over, either. But occasionally, you may see the lights in your mirror, look around, and not see an obvious place to pull over. You might be concerned with your safety, or with blocking traffic, or with the quality of the neighborhood. Most of that doesn't matter. When a cop tells you to stop, you stop.

LEGAL BRIEFS: Choosing a better place to stop after the officer signals to you, may make *you* feel a little safer, but it's probably going to piss off the officer and put him on edge.

But there may be a time when you're not willing to do so, for whatever reason, and you choose to select a better spot. Beware: Doing so may make *you* feel a little safer, but it's probably going to piss off the officer and put him on edge.

First and foremost, be cognizant of your mirrors. Safety experts recommend that riders check their mirrors at least every seven seconds in heavy traffic and every 14 to 20 seconds in light traffic or rural areas. But it's common that motorcyclists, paying close attention to what's going on in front of them (much,

much more important statistically than what's going on behind them!), forget about their mirrors and ride along with the flow of traffic, oblivious of the cop car and flashing lights behind them. If you have a helmet on and are wearing earplugs, you probably can't hear the police car, either—all you get is bike noise and wind noise. Regardless of whether you know he's there or not, a police officer may interpret your behavior as that of a troublemaker. He sees it as disregarding a direct order from a police officer. He is suddenly put on alert, because he figures you *do* know he's there and you're thinking about whether or not to run.

This exact situation happened to me several years ago. The riding environment was heavy: 45-mph morning rush hour traffic; two lanes in each direction separated by a tree-lined boulevard, with no shoulder. A roadside city cop's radar lit up with 50-plus mph, and he zeroed in on me out of all the other vehicles. Officer Mike pulled out, hit his lights, and attempted to stop me.

Meanwhile, I was in the right lane at 45, with traffic slowly proceeding past me on the left at 50 or so, carefully watching what was going on up ahead but more or less sleepy and indifferent to my routine commute. I had no reason to think I wouldn't be at my desk in 10 minutes. I was wearing a full-faced helmet with foam earplugs—plus a red Aerostich suit, gloves, boots, and courier bag.

Suddenly, the guy in the car ahead of me hit his brakes for no reason, and I decided I no longer wanted to follow that vehicle. I passed the car and returned to the right lane. After the pass, I glanced in the mirror only to see an unmarked gray cruiser with lights flashing behind me, and I realized at the same time he was also using his sirens and loudspeaker to try to get my attention. By this time, no matter what I was doing right or wrong, I already had a pissed-off cop who thought I was going to run. Great.

LEGAL BRIEFS: If there's no safe place to pull over, at least acknowledge the officer by putting a hand out, track-exit style or left-turn style, and try to keep it there as long as it's safe to do so.

Problem was, the traffic was heavy and there was no place to pull over without blocking half the road. Being overly concerned with holding up the flow, I continued along at 45 because I knew there was a place to turn off about a mile up the road. Bad idea for me. The cop just kept getting angrier and angrier. By the time I did pull over, and he got out of his car, he had his hand on the butt of his gun, and he was ready for the worst. *Don't let this happen to you.*

Unless you genuinely fear for your safety at the roadside, pull your bike over and turn it off. Don't worry about holding up traffic. But, if there's no safe place to pull over, at least acknowledge the officer by putting a hand out, track-exit style or left-turn style, and try to keep it there as long as it's safe to do so. This shows the cop that you are aware of his request, and it also sort of evokes the TV-style submission posture of "hands up!" when someone has a gun pointed at them. At any rate, a rider sitting bolt upright with one hand in the air should be perceived as less of a threat than a rider who just downshifted, crouched down, and started weaving in and out of traffic. Now, find a place to stop as quickly as possible.

Choose a place that's highly visible to other people, well out of the way from traffic flow, and free of surface hazards or a downward slope. At night, it's a good idea to choose an area that is well lit. You want to find an exit ramp, side street, driveway, parking lot, or shoulder area that's level and has a solid surface that's free of gravel, mud, broken pavement, and debris. Be careful to select a spot that provides good visibility for the police officer and other motorists—not just over the crest of a hill or around a sharp curve. Avoid areas with a guardrail that would prevent you or the officer from positioning yourself a safe distance off the road. Try to select a spot that has plenty of room for both you and the cop car.

Also consider factors that affect the safety of the police officer. Remember: That cop's goal is to go home at the end of his shift, and he's trained to make sure it happens. If you're stopped on a road with a high speed limit and there is heavy traffic, this presents a potentially dangerous situation. Be mindful that the officer will want to see your hands—don't immediately start digging for your license and registration. Wait until he or she directs you to do so. If you're traveling in a group, it may make the situation tenser for a police officer than if you're riding alone. Don't get off your bike until you're asked to do so. Expect the officer to approach you from the right side of your bike, rather than the left, if there is a lot of traffic.

LEGAL BRIEFS: Be mindful that the officer will want to see your hands—don't immediately start digging for your license and registration.

PUTTING THE POLICE OFFICER AT EASE

Cooperate, use the terms "yes, sir" and "no, sir" (or "ma'am"), and provide the information you're asked for. Do not be angry with the cop

LEGAL BRIEFS: **When pulled over, turn off the bike, remain seated, and place your ignition key on the tank.**

for pulling you over. She is just doing her job. She is not out having fun like you are.

Turn off the bike, remain seated, and place your ignition key on the tank. If you're riding a bike that has the ignition key under the tank or seat, or somewhere else, use the engine cutoff switch on the handlebar instead to turn off the engine—leaving the headlight on. Immediately let the officer know the ignition key is under the tank and that you would like to reach down to turn it off.

Keep your hands visible, put the sidestand down, lean the bike over to a parked position, and turn the handlebars to the left, without dismounting. Many police officers are overly concerned that a rider will attempt to flee, and effectively "parking" the motorcycle will make it appear less likely that you will do that. Expect that the officer will want you to dismount and move away from the bike.

If you're wearing a helmet and/or earplugs and the only thing you can hear is your own voice, you need to get the officer's attention and clearly inform him that you cannot hear anything he says and need to remove your gear in order to communicate. *You need to be clear about this and get the lines of communication open before anything else.* Police officers are trained to deal with citizens with all sorts of disabilities, and they likely understand how to treat someone with a hearing problem. But they don't realize you can't hear them until you point it out to them.

"Sir, do you know how fast you were going?"

"Excuse me, ma'am: I am wearing earplugs under my helmet. I cannot hear anything you say until I take them off. Is it okay if I take off my helmet and take out my earplugs so I can hear you?"

This will show the officer that you're at a disadvantage but want to be able to communicate, and it will put him or her more at ease. However, if you can hear okay, or you're wearing a half- or three-quarter helmet, you should consider leaving the helmet on. It is possible that some officers may view a helmet in a rider's hands as a potential weapon. (Also, leaving a full-faced helmet on during a stop-and-cite might give you a defense later in court, when you ask the officer how he knew the person he stopped was you.)

Most cops won't perceive a helmet as a weapon. Taking your helmet off and holding it keeps your hands busy so they can't be doing other things like retrieving weapons or tossing drugs into the bushes. Taking your helmet off also allows the officer to see your face clearly, which will allow him to better assess the person he's dealing with, and it reassures him that you're not preparing to flee. Explain to the officer that you placed the key on the tank, and ask him if it's okay to put it in your pocket. (They like that.)

If it's hot, and you need to get off the bike and remove your gloves and jacket before you melt, be sure you ask the officer first if it's okay to do so.

LEGAL BRIEFS: **Most cops won't perceive a helmet as a weapon. Taking your helmet off also allows the officer to see your face clearly, which will allow him to better assess the person he's dealing with, and it reassures him that you're not preparing to flee.**

"Sir, it's really hot in all this riding gear sitting on a hot motorcycle. Is it okay if I hop off and remove my jacket?"

This can be a mixed bag for a police officer. On one hand, you're off the bike so you're less likely to initiate a high-speed chase. On the other hand, it puts you in greater physical proximity to start trouble or assault the officer. Keep your hands visible and maintain a respectful distance, whatever you do.

When asked for your license and insurance cards, you will probably need to remind the police officer clearly and carefully that you have to dig it out of your jacket, from under your seat, or from your tank bag or backpack. Cops are not immediately aware that motorcyclists can't just reach into the glove compartment and pull out a registration card and can't just whip out a wallet to show a driver's license. That stuff is usually buried somewhere, and law enforcement doesn't like it when stopped motorists go searching for buried treasure. Tell them exactly where the items are located, and clearly ask permission to retrieve them.

> LEGAL BRIEFS: **When asked for your license and insurance cards, you will probably need to remind the police officer clearly and carefully that you have to dig it out of your jacket, from under your seat, or from your tank bag or backpack.**

"Sir, my driver's license is in my back pocket, and I have to dig into my riding suit to get it. My insurance card is in storage under the passenger seat. I'll need to remove the passenger seat to get it. That will require that I use my key. I want you to know that under the passenger seat is also a tool kit wrapped in a black bag and an electric tire pump."

If you can, always try to carry your license, proof of insurance, and registration information or cab card somewhere that's easily accessible without a lot of mysterious monkeying around.

If you carry a weapon, be absolutely certain you store it somewhere away from your documents. That way it doesn't appear you're about to pull a gun instead of an insurance card. And if you do have weapons on the bike, inform the officer what they are and where they are located as well as their status (such as loaded or unloaded). Expect this new information to put the officer even more on alert.

WHAT TO SAY AND WHAT NOT TO SAY

If the officer asks you any questions, answer honestly but never admit guilt. Answer only the questions you are asked. What you say at a roadside stop can be used against you in a moving violation prosecution, so don't give the officer any evidence if you can help it. In fact, remaining rather mute and accepting a ticket is an often-used strategy when you intend to fight that ticket down the line. Being argumentative and saying "I'll see you in court" will probably only make things more complicated.

"Mr. Hahn, do you know why I pulled you over?"

"No, ma'am, I don't."

"Mr. Hahn, do you know what the speed limit is?"

"Yes, ma'am, the speed limit is 45."

> LEGAL BRIEFS: **If the officer asks you any questions, answer honestly but never admit guilt.**

"Mr. Hahn, do you know how fast you were going?"

"I don't know."

Or you could say, "I don't know. I was focused on riding with the flow of traffic."

Or: "I believe I was going the speed limit."

Or you could say, "I believe I was going the speed limit, because I was riding with the flow of traffic."

Or: "I checked my speedometer before you pulled me over and I was going 45."

All of these responses demonstrate in their own way that you're being honest, while at the same time not admitting you were knowingly breaking any laws.

There are a couple approaches to roadside stops concerning what to say and what not to say. If you're trying to escape a ticket entirely, relying on your friendly nature, pretty face, or a lifetime of constabulary good luck, consider engaging the officer in friendly conversation, explanation, or even admission that you weren't paying close enough attention. However, be careful of admitting your guilt.

"I might have been speeding, but I wasn't aware of it because I was concerned about the truck following me so closely."

"I might have been speeding. I just left the interstate and have been whipping along at 70 all day. My brain might not have registered that it was now 55."

Sometimes a cop has no intention of writing you a ticket and just wants to let you know that it's his turf and he's serious about traffic safety. He checks to make sure you're not drunk or a wanted criminal, tells you to slow down, and sends you on your way. But if this good-natured cop thinks you're lying to him or playing a game with him, he might change his mind. Honesty and submission can go a long way to getting you a warning instead of a citation.

However, if you are certain you're getting a ticket and you intend to fight it, the best advice is to keep quiet. Only answer the questions you're asked, and don't admit you broke any laws. Also, don't say anything that might help the officer remember you, the conversation, or anything else about the stop—though you could consider asking the officer a few questions of your own.

"Why did you pull me over?"

"How did you determine I was speeding?"

"Where was I when you determined I was speeding?"

"May I see the radar/laser reading?"

But questions like these will probably indicate to the officer that you're a ticket fighter, and he'll start documenting everything he can so that he's prepared when the court hearing comes.

This is good advice *now*, well after the fact, concerning that day long ago when I was pulled over by Officer Mike. This all went very badly for me when I finally was able to pull over. By the time I had stopped, the officer was very angry. It appeared to him that I was trying to run. Then, when he finally was able to get out of the car and talk to me, I couldn't hear him due to the helmet, earplugs, and traffic going by. This made it worse. He was yelling at me and issuing orders, and I started getting angry because I couldn't hear him and had no idea why he pulled me over or why he was so pissed off. I yanked off my helmet and ripped out my earplugs, my adrenaline percolating and ready for fight-or-flight. Don't think he didn't notice that! We yelled at each other a bit, and then—when I angrily stuffed my hand into my suit to grab my license (buried under my suit) and ripped open my inner pocket to get at my insurance card—he nearly pulled his gun on me.

It was only after having me in handcuffs in the back of his car that he started to calm down. He looked up my (clean) driving record and was surprised to see that I didn't have a history of fleeing the police. I explained to him that I wasn't speeding and that I wasn't trying to run. I tried to tell him that I simply didn't realize he was even there, and when I finally figured it out, I was then trying to find a safe place to pull over so we didn't hold up traffic for two miles. His response was to write me citations for speeding and inattentive driving and give me a lecture about pulling over when I'm told to.

We'll come back to this story again in the next chapter, "Fighting a Ticket."

GOOD RESOURCE

National Police Car Archives: http://policecararchives.org

4

Fighting a Ticket

WHY FIGHT?

There are plenty of reasons to fight a traffic ticket in court. The most important reason, of course, is to keep your driving record clean and your driving privileges intact. But there are other reasons too.

IT'S YOUR RIGHT TO DO SO

Not to get all uppity, but the United States is a country in which its citizens are innocent until proven guilty. You have a right to face your accuser no matter what the crime, hear him or her try to prove you committed the crime, and defend yourself against false accusations.

IT'S YOUR CIVIC DUTY TO DO SO

We live in a participatory democracy. Most of us have very few opportunities to participate directly in our government's process unless we're employed as a civil servant, legislator, police officer, or judge. But standing up for yourself in court is one way for an ordinary citizen to participate. Jury duty is another. Attending a city council or school board meeting is another. These activities are rarely "fun," but it's important that the people running the show do not do so in a complete vacuum and without regard to the people they serve.

We are given the opportunity to vote for our elected officials. You remember from high school civics class that you should do so with great energy and pride, even if you don't give a whit who the candidates are. You should approach fighting tickets the same way.

IT'S YOUR SOCIAL DUTY TO DO SO

Writing traffic tickets, for law enforcement, has got to be like catching fish in a barrel. Motorists are easy prey. We're required to stop when they tell us to. We're required to provide our identification or submit to a breath test when they tell us to. We're required to show them our paperwork when they tell us to. And there are so many laws on the books that it's got to be nearly impossible to operate a vehicle without violating one law or another. An ambitious ticket writer just has to figure out exactly which law it was that you violated. Writing tickets has got to be way easier than investigating and prosecuting misdemeanor or felony crimes.

It's your social duty, to your neighbors and fellow citizens everywhere, to make writing tickets more difficult by making the process more work for law enforcement and the judiciary and less profitable to the cities, counties, and states that take your money. Fewer than one in 10 motorists are willing to fight a traffic ticket in court. Most of us just knuckle under and pay the fine to have the whole thing over with, whether we're guilty of what we're accused of or not. Fact is, it's easier for most of us just to pay the fine and get on with our lives than it is to stand up for ourselves.

But standing up and fighting accomplishes two important things, one short term and one long term. First, you have an opportunity to defend yourself against an accusation and clear your name and driving record of any wrongdoing. Second, by doing so and winning, you've just made law enforcement slightly less likely to write that sort of ticket. You've tied up a police officer and court clerk, prosecutor, and judge for the duration of your hearing, costing the state money. (It costs you nothing to have your day in court, but it costs the court plenty. The most you'll have to pay is the fine on the ticket you're contesting.) You've made the type of ticket you received slightly less profitable for police officers to write and courts to prosecute. And you've opened the door for others to follow suit and fight their own tickets.

LEGAL BRIEFS: Fewer than one in 10 motorists are willing to fight a traffic ticket in court.

Instead of one in 10, can you imagine if nine out of 10 citizens fought every ticket they received? There would be no cops on the road, because they'd all be in court all the time waiting to testify against motorists. There would be less room on the docket to prosecute more critical misdemeanor and felony crimes because the court would be tied up trying to prosecute $25 parking tickets or $100 speeding tickets. What populace would tolerate a court tied up with nickel-and-dime traffic tickets when they should be prosecuting drunk drivers and armed robbers and Ponzi schemers?

LEGAL BRIEFS: By going to court, unless you do something really dumb like lie under oath or infuriate the judge, the worst that will happen is you'll have to pay the fine that you would have paid anyway.

YOU DIDN'T EARN THE TICKET

All these reasons should be good enough already, but here's the big one: You didn't do what the cop said you did. If you've been following the advice in this book and obeying the law and keeping your head down, the ticket you just received was issued to you in error. You know the rules, and you follow them, which means the police officer who cited you for whatever violation made a mistake. Maybe his mistake was in how he used his speed measurement device. Maybe his mistake was pulling over a vehicle that looked just like yours a few minutes after he witnessed the violation. Maybe his understanding of the law he's accusing you of violating isn't as good as it should be. No matter what, if you didn't earn it, there is no way in hell you should pay for it.

No matter what, it's worth it to take your ticket to court. Unless you do something really dumb like lie under oath or infuriate the judge, the worst that will happen is you'll have to pay the fine that you would have paid anyway. You're out nothing, and you had the opportunity to participate in the process and make a good stab at fighting for your rights.

ANGLE OF ATTACK

Of course, and obviously, fighting a ticket is easier said than done. Getting a ticket, and fighting a ticket, costs you time and/or money. If you don't have time and/or money to devote to the process, don't break the law . . . or don't let yourself get put in a situation where you're accused of something you didn't do. The whole process from start to finish is set up to discourage you at every turn for standing up for yourself. It's just so much easier to cave in and pay.

All of the reasons cited for fighting a ticket are on the more "noble" end of the spectrum. They're bonuses—nice features but, really, who has the time for all that? Where the rubber meets the road, though, is where your desire to have a clean record ends and your time and money begin. No one except for maybe an eccentric, unemployed, millionaire libertarian is going to fight every traffic violation to within an inch of his life because that's the way it should be. You're not that guy. Your goal is simply to keep your record clean.

For the purposes of this book and for the rest of the chapter, we're going to operate under the assumption that you don't care about any of that noble stuff—you are a practical, mostly law-abiding motorist, and you just want the whole thing to be over and for the end result to be you hanging onto your clean driving record. Therefore, your angle of attack is going to be one of *compromise*: Do only what you have to in order to get the result you want. You don't have to win the fight 100 percent; you just have to get what you want: a clean record with minimal time and hassle.

What you have to do will vary depending on what you did and who you're facing in the courtroom, so we'll take it in steps. There are three levels of fighting tickets, each with its own measure of effort required and chances of success:

- **Level One: Convince the Clerk. This takes very little effort, and if your record's clean, you stand a good chance of being successful.**
- **Level Two: Convince the Prosecutor. This takes quite a bit more effort. Again, if your record's clean, you stand a halfway decent chance of being successful.**
- **Level Three: Convince the Judge. This requires a great deal of effort, and your success depends not only on whether you did what they're saying you did but also on whether you are able to cast reasonable doubt in the judge's mind about whether you did what they're saying you did.**

OUR MODEST GOAL

The simplest and cheapest way to keep your record clean is to pay to have your ticket dismissed. This is Level One. Our goal is never, ever to have to move beyond this point. But here is the first act of compromise on your part. Even if you didn't do what they're saying you did, you're still going to pay the fine in exchange for keeping the citation off your driving record. A traffic fine is minimal compared to the hit you'd eventually take on your insurance premiums. And a conviction on your driving record becomes even more expensive, theoretically, when and if you someday receive another citation: The court would be less likely to dismiss a ticket written to someone with a history of breaking the law.

LEGAL BRIEFS:
The simplest and cheapest way to keep your record clean is to pay to have your ticket dismissed.

Also, a conviction on your record makes it more difficult to be able to wiggle out of future citations, which makes it more likely that you'd end up getting your license suspended someday for having too many convictions within too short a window of time.

This process of paying to have your ticket dismissed goes by many names. Sometimes what you're looking for is called a "continuance for dismissal." Other times it's referred to as "probation before judgment." Whatever it's called, it is the act of negotiating with the court either to drop or postpone prosecuting your violation in exchange for giving them what they really want: your money.

LEVEL ZERO

Before we go through the process of fighting a ticket from Level One through Level Three, we need to establish the strategy for every traffic stop that will help you in each one of those stages. You read the last chapter, so you already know how to keep the traffic stop process safe and efficient. Now you need to look at it from a strategic perspective: What do I need to do to maximize my chances of success in court? In one sentence, what you need to do is avoid giving the cop any reason to remember you.

I came across one story that illustrates this point very well. A long time ago, a rider was cited for an improper horn—the squeezy type that sounds more like a goose than a motorcycle. He was also cited for going 60 in a 40. During the process, he was unable to keep his mouth shut and made it a special point to challenge and irritate the police officer. The six companions he was traveling with that day each had their ticket dismissed when the officer did not show up to court. However, the officer made it a special point to show up for this fellow's hearing, and both tickets stuck. A little humility and a zipper on your mouth can go a long way in helping you fight your ticket.

What you can get away with in one state or regional area may be very different from what you can get away with somewhere else. And there are a fair number of things you can never get away with, such as speeding in a school zone or residential area, blowing off a stopped and flashing school bus, and passing on a double yellow. It's also difficult to get away with much when a cop may be particularly motivated—perhaps at month's end or year's end, or perhaps at the end of an enforcement wave or fiscal year. There is good research that shows that enforcement works—that it saves lives and reduces injuries—and a lot of money pours into states from the federal government to enforce speeding and impaired-driving laws.

Very few approaches on the side of the road can get you out of a ticket if the cop is of a mind to write one. Pretending you have no idea why you were pulled over isn't going to fool anyone if you were clearly doing it. Welling up with alligator tears has been done to death. Every traffic cop has a similar story that starts with "some lady bawling her eyes out" and ends with "the minute I handed her the ticket, the tears disappeared and she instantly turned into a complete, hostile you-know-what." They've all heard the "I had to go to the bathroom" one before. However, if the cop was recently in the same situation (on the road with no relief in sight), he or she might be a little more sympathetic—especially if you ask right away if you can run into the bushes and take care of business. Yet this does violate the first rule, which is to not give the cop any reason to remember you, so only use it if you have a, er, pressing need to do so.

"I was going with the flow" (pun intended) is a weak argument and rarely works. Compare it to a referee throwing a flag in a football game or assigning a penalty in a basketball game: These violations are happening everywhere, all the time, and it takes a little something extra—maybe in the ref's mind, maybe in the situation, maybe in your behavior—to get you noticed and penalized. It never matters if everybody else was doing it too. You did it, and you have to take responsibility for it—and be smarter about keeping it low profile in the future.

Cops have excellent built-in bullshit detectors. Don't try to BS the cop or come up with some lame or outlandish excuse for why you did what he says you did. It's always best to keep quiet and let him do his job. You can be silent and be honest at the same time. Be polite and cooperative, rather than argumentative and nitpicking. Being nice may get you a reduced citation (maybe he writes you up for your missing mirror rather than a speeding ticket). Being belligerent and disobedient means he's going to do everything he can to wreck your day.

At the roadside, there is always a chance that you'll end up with a warning instead of a citation. So during the stop, listen quietly to the cop's lecture if he chooses to give you one. If the cop feels like he's getting his point across, and that you agree that the job of highway safety is important, he might let you off with a warning. This is not the time for conversation, however. In case you do get a ticket, anything you say might lodge in his memory and give him more ammunition down the line in the courtroom. Never, ever admit you were doing what the cop thinks you were doing—a statement like that will prove the state's case in court. "Yeah, I know I was speeding, but I really had to use the bathroom."

It is okay, and even sometimes necessary for your case, to verify how the police officer determined you broke the law. But don't bother to ask the cop if you can see the radar/laser. What you see won't make a difference anyway—he or she could have zeroed out the unit already, and safety precautions dictate that they don't have to show it to you anyway. Don't stick around after you've received your ticket. Calmly and coolly get out of there.

You may be asked to sign the citation. This is not an admission of guilt, but rather an acknowledgement that you received the ticket and are aware of your responsibility (of either paying the ticket by the due date or showing up in court). However, if you're unsure, it's okay to double-check with the officer

LEGAL BRIEFS: **Cops have excellent built-in bullshit detectors. Don't try to BS the cop or come up with some lame or outlandish excuse for why you did what he says you did.**

whether signing it means you're pleading guilty or not. Note that refusing to sign the citation can lead to your arrest, so don't get too worked up about it. And causing a problem over a minor administrative point will make you much more memorable.

GATHERING INFORMATION

We're going to work under the assumption that you're a law-abiding rider and you were written a ticket in error. There had to be some mistake, otherwise you wouldn't have gotten a ticket, correct? The mistake could have been anything, from the cop's interpretation of the law to her use of speed measurement equipment to mistaking your bike for the one she had originally set out to pursue. To be convicted of a crime, even a minor crime like a moving violation, you have to have broken the law exactly as it reads, which usually involves many variables that add up to an actual violation. If you didn't commit the infraction, then one or more of those variables will turn out to be incorrect. Find it and use it.

You'll want to look at the traffic stop from every angle to figure out what went wrong. But don't do it right away. If the cop sees you documenting everything, she'll sense that you're a ticket fighter and start strengthening her case by making lots of notes about you. Come back and make notes, draw diagrams, and take photos as soon as you can after the cop leaves the scene. You'll want to document a whole slew of variables that you may need later if you get to the point where have to prove your innocence to a judge:

- **What was the roadway type? Two-lane, four-lane, divided, controlled-access?**
- **What were the roadway characteristics? Straight, curved, twisting, hilly, rural, suburban, urban?**
- **What were the roadside characteristics? Wide-open, clustered with buildings, vegetation?**
- **What was the traffic like? Thick, thin, nonexistent?**
- **What other vehicles were near your vehicle when you supposedly broke the law?**
- **What was the speed limit? Had it recently changed, or was it just about to change to a different speed? Where was the last speed limit sign? Was it visible?**

- What other signs were there?
- What time of day was it? What was the weather and visibility like? Where was the sun?
- Where did you stop your vehicle? Where did the cop stop his/her vehicle?
- Where were you when you first identified the police officer who pulled you over?
- Where were you when the police officer decided to pull you over?
- Where were you when the police officer decided you broke the law? Was his or her view of you clear from the initial decision to the time you were pulled over?
- How did the police officer determine you broke the law?

Compare all these things to the information on your ticket to make sure that what is on the ticket is not inaccurate, and make notes of any discrepancies. Go find the spot where the officer first saw you and take photos and notes there about what that officer could and could not see.

Know your citation and look up the language of the law you were cited under. Is it correct? How is a violation defined exactly? Is it accurate? Make sure all the numbers, letters, color of vehicle, descriptions, etc., are correct. Read the ticket carefully to make sure you understand what's expected of you and what the cop will be testifying to in court, if it gets that far. Any inaccuracies there could work out to your advantage. Maybe the vehicle description is wrong, suggesting that the officer pulled over a red bike but not necessarily the red bike he saw breaking the law. Maybe the street name is wrong, suggesting that you're now so far away from the "scene of the crime" that the cop has mistaken you for someone else.

LEGAL BRIEFS: **To be convicted of a crime, even a minor crime like a moving violation, you have to have broken the law exactly as it reads, which usually involves many variables that add up to an actual violation.**

Look up the statute or administrative code under which you were cited, and carefully analyze the language. There will be one, or many, criteria for a violation that will need to be satisfied by the prosecution in order to make the ticket stick. Pick it apart and interpret the language carefully until you find the smoking gun. For example, when the cop says you didn't come to a complete stop at a stop sign because you didn't put your feet down, you can question where in the law it says that at stop signs motorcyclists must put their feet down. If your ticket was issued by a robot (a speed or red light camera), find out what the requirements are for a conviction and whether or not a conviction carries any points.

The order in which you take your ticket fight is 1) court clerk, 2) prosecutor, and then 3) judge. Hopefully, you can beat your ticket without ever reaching the judge. Your goal is to get a continuance for dismissal, probation before judgment. If your record is clean and your citation came from a larger metropolitan jurisdiction, chances are you can get a continuance from the clerk. Expect this to cost you 50 to 150 percent of the dollar amount on your citation for court costs.

LEVEL ONE

The goal of Level One is to get your ticket dismissed without having to make a court appearance, do any research, or take any time off work or away from your life. The basic premise is that you go into the courthouse and offer to pay the fine immediately if they'll dismiss the ticket. If your record is clean, most of the time this works.

In metropolitan areas, there are people employed to deal with this kind of approach. The volume they manage for license reinstatements, revocations, hearings, administration, and court appearances makes it easy to justify having someone handle just the slam dunks—the probation-before judgments for individuals who receive citations but also have clean records. Big city courts don't want to waste their time with these, so they appoint civil servants to act on the judge's behalf for the easy cases.

In smaller burghs, the volume they deal with is quite a bit less and they're therefore less apt just to throw out a ticket because your driving record is good, but it's still worth a try. You were written the ticket in error,

> **LEGAL BRIEFS: The basic premise is that you go into the courthouse and offer to pay the fine immediately if they'll dismiss the ticket. If your record is clean, most of the time this works.**

and you'll have no choice but to fight it. But to avoid having to take time off work and time away from your life and pull everything together like an amateur lawyer, you're willing just to give them their money if they'll keep the citation off your driving record. They honestly do not care about whether or not they leave a mark on your driving record unless you're a local menace.

So, before payment of your fine is due, go to the courthouse and talk to the clerk. Put on an air of frustrated taxpayer (doing the right thing and simultaneously bewildered by it all) and ask to speak with someone about your ticket. Here's an example of how it might go:

"Ma'am, can I help you?"

"Yes, I'd like to speak to someone about a traffic ticket I received."

"That'd be me. What's your driver's license number?"

(Tappity-tap on the keyboard and your driving record pops up.)

"Okay, what can we do for you?"

"I was given this ticket for speeding, but I was not speeding. I don't know why I was given this ticket. But I know better than to argue with a police officer on the side of the road, so I thought I'd clear it up this way."

"Well, [based on your clean driving record] here's what we can do. We'll dismiss this ticket as long as you get no same or similar tickets in the next 12 months. If you get another speeding ticket, not only will that one count but this one will count, too."

"Aw gee, that's great. I really appreciate it."

"There is the small matter of the bill. To do this, you need to pay our fifeeen-dollar administrative fee and one-hundred-and-twenty-five-dollar county surcharge. You can pay the cashier out front on your way out. Have a nice day."

"Aw gee, that's swell."

This is almost exactly the way it shook out when I went to the courthouse after my run-in with Officer Mike. I picked a midweek day and went in about 10 in the morning. I waited quite a while in a room filled with people trying to solve various court-related problems. Seeing the volume of folks there and guessing there was only one person handling them all, I began to lose my optimism. But I hung in there.

When I was finally called in, the guy behind the desk seemed almost relieved that I was just coming to discuss a traffic citation. Well, two of them actually. I did my best to play confused, concerned citizen trying to correct what must be a common mistake. It went something like this:

"What can we do for you today?"

"I got this ticket but I wasn't speeding. I don't know what happened."

(The clerk looked at ticket then started tapping away at keyboard. I continued while he was typing.)

"It was a busy morning and this police officer, Officer Mike, pulled me over and was really, really mad at me. I had no idea what I did wrong. I was afraid he was going to shoot me. He wrote me tickets for speeding and 'inattentive driving,' whatever that is."

"Yeah, we all know Officer Mike." (Laughs.)

After a little more typing, the clerk offered me a continuance for dismissal. "Based on your driving record I can dismiss these tickets as long as you don't get another similar type of ticket in the next year. Fair enough?"

"Thanks, I really appreciate that."

"You won't have to pay the fine, but you will have to pay the administrative fee of one-hundred-and-thirty-five-dollars." (I got a two-fer! I think one ticket dismissal would have cost me the same amount. Both tickets together, if I'd paid the fines, were somewhere in the $275 range.)

"That's just fine, I appreciate the quick service."

And like that, I was in the clear as long as I didn't screw up again in the next year.

So when you get dismissed this way, the problem is solved and the points you dread are gone, but here is the rub—a continuance is only good if you're generally a law-abider (or really, really good at fighting tickets). You get to keep the points off your record in exchange for your promise of good driving behavior. If you screw up again, you'll be looking at two tickets—much more difficult to fight simultaneously than one at a time. Let's say you get probation before judgment for a speeding ticket, 50 in a 40. You go in, look all bewildered, and say it was a mistake and they let you off the hook—once. Then, six months later you get another ticket.

When you go in and tell them again that the ticket was written in error, even though the points never hit your driving record, the citation is still there for another six months. Now they'll be less likely to cut a deal with you right away.

LEGAL BRIEFS: **The lesson is, if you get a continuance for dismissal, you have to make damn sure you don't get tangled up in another ticket before the probation ends.**

The lesson is, if you get a continuance for dismissal, you have to make damn sure you don't get tangled up in another ticket before the probation ends.

Here's why it's also important that you understand the consequences of the charge against you. If it's just a minor infraction that won't cost you any points on your driving record (like a parking ticket or an equipment violation), it's often more efficient just to pay it and get it out of your life. However, those of us in the clean-record business appreciate your willingness to go the extra mile just on principle.

If you don't get what you want from the clerk, the next step is to convince the prosecutor that it's easier to give you a continuance for dismissal. Ask to schedule a court date.

LEVEL TWO

For whatever reason, if you're not able to sweep this whole traffic ticket thing under the rug in Level One, it's time to move on to Level Two. Rats.

The amount of work involved in Level Two is not twice as much as Level One—it's 10 times as much. Twenty maybe. Make your Level One efforts count. Don't ever get to Level Two if you don't have to. Here your goal is to prepare your case as much as possible without showing your hand to the court—maintain your uneducated innocence. You need to have a plan, a reason why you're special, but you don't have to reveal it to anybody. It's still a good idea to come off like a rookie, like you've never heard about any of this before, like you have no intention of going toe to toe with a seasoned prosecutor. You want to keep them sleepy and unwary of your approach.

Level Two requires you to plan to take at least one day out of your life simply to participate in the process. Plan to take several hours (or days) to do the research necessary to participate in the process. And hope like hell that all this research and the turns of phrase you will soon be able to use are enough to get the prosecutor to agree that yes, you were issued a ticket in error—and yes, we can work out a deal with you.

The point of Level Two is to figure out why you were issued the ticket in error and point it out to the prosecutor before you have to go in front of a judge. The prosecutor is a busy guy or gal. He or she has important stuff to work on, and some otherwise law-abiding citizen who's miffed he got an undeserved traffic ticket is the least of his or her worries—and the least of the city's worries, when it comes to public safety. See if you can get a hearing with the prosecutor before the court date.

"Yes?"

"I didn't earn this ticket. There was no way I did that."

"Okay, so what do you want me to do about it?"

"Drop it."

"I can't do that. I haven't even heard the police officer's side of the story."

"Look, I don't want a fight. I have a clean driving record and my goal is to keep it that way. I'm willing to pay the fine in order to keep the ticket off my record." (Use the informal term *ticket* rather than *citation* or *conviction*.)

"Well, here's what I can do at this point. You can plead guilty to a nine-over speeding ticket instead of ten-over, which means the ticket won't go on your record. How's that?"

"I appreciate that. Where do I pay?"

Or: "Well, here's what I can do at this point. You can plead guilty to the speeding ticket, but we'll leave it off your driving record if you pay the fine and take a driver improvement clinic, which costs about one hundred fifty dollars."

"I appreciate that. Where do I pay?"

If you can get in to see the prosecutor before your court hearing, you don't need to work all that hard to do your research and build your case. Just having a specific memory and reason for your visit is good enough, although it helps to be fluent in the rule or statute you're cited under and have a good explanation why it doesn't apply to you. It's a lot easier to speak with an attorney informally than it is to stand up there in front of a judge and act like Perry Mason.

SO HOW DO I DO IT?

Track down every last bit of information about the date, day, time, weather, traffic, violation, statute, and roadside interaction you can so you have a scientific, computer-like view of the whole sordid event. You have to look at your lawbreaking like Aristotle or Sir Isaac Newton, not Lindsay Lohan. Then, focus primarily on the variable (or variables) that proves you did not commit the violation, or at least those variables that can cast reasonable doubt on the assumption that you are guilty. For example:

LEGAL BRIEFS: Track down every last bit of information about the date, day, time, weather, traffic, violation, statute, and roadside interaction you can so you have a scientific, computer-like view of the whole sordid event.

The police officer checked you on radar at 50 in a 40. "Well, the speed limit where he checked me was still 50."

The police officer checked you on radar at 50 in a 40. "Well, I was doing 40 when a car passed me at 50. Maybe the radar read the wrong vehicle."

The police officer checked you on radar at 50 in a 40. "Well, maybe that other rider on a blue motorcycle was the one who was doing 50. I was doing 40."

And on and on. The point is that the statute under which you were cited is very, very specific. They all are. It will state that to be guilty of violation A, you have to have perpetrated actions W, X, Y, and Z. All you have to do is analyze the statute, and the language of the statute, and the reason you're not guilty will appear before you as if by magic. For example, I once decided to stretch and flex a little bit on a rural in-town road marked 30 mph. After 80 or so miles on twisty back roads, I loosened up by swerving around in my lane a bit while we were putzing through town—to impress the riders behind me and to burn off steam and energy. Well, the local prepubescent cop decided to write me a ticket for it: unsafe lane deviation. I went to the state website and looked up the statute and it turned out I had to leave my lane of travel to be guilty of it. Wham, bam! After one statement from an eyewitness (the embarrassed rider behind me) and a quick trip to the courthouse to talk to the prosecutor, I was on my way.

DISCOVERY

Don't bother with requesting "discovery" at this point. Discovery is the act of requesting the state's documentation of your violation: any evidence they can use against you. It's a pain in the ass for the state to provide it for a stupid $100 stop sign violation, which won't get you any favors or preferable treatment. And there's nothing they'll provide that you don't already know (or couldn't have figured out on your own) anyway. Worst, it'll tip the prosecutor off that you're preparing to go to the wall over this citation—or that you enjoy being a freedom-fighter cum liberty-preserving amateur lawyer. If she is in a fighting mood, she'll do the extra work (reading the ticket, talking to the police officer beforehand and prepping him, getting familiar with your driving record) to stick it to you and show you who's boss. Instead of showing your hand right away, skip the discovery process and let 'em wonder.

LEVEL THREE

Any way you look at it, a continuation or plea bargain in which you pay some or your entire fine and nothing shows up on your record is a win-win situation for both you and the court.

If you can't achieve this, the next step is to go to court and try to get the case dismissed. If you can't get it dismissed before a court hearing, you'll have to try to beat the ticket based on facts and evidence. This is Level Three. If you are certain you are right, and the judge finds you guilty anyway, you can always appeal the decision. On your way out of the courtroom, ask the cashier how to do this. It is likely that an appeal will cost you additional money. Hiring a lawyer for this process is recommended.

DISCOVERY, AGAIN

At this point you probably want to request "discovery" to see the evidence the state has against you. However, due to the labor involved on the court's side, this may not be granted in low-level court hearings—and may be immediate grounds for dismissal when you tell it to the judge. Not only do you have a right to a speedy trial, you have a right to review any information that can be submitted as evidence in court. If the court does not afford you these rights, any judge worth his or her salt will not only ask why but also send you on your way. It is possible that the judge will postpone the trial at the last minute in order for the court to provide

LEGAL BRIEFS: **Any way you look at it, a continuation or plea bargain in which you pay some or your entire fine and nothing shows up on your record is a win-win situation for both you and the court.**

you this information, but then they run the risk of not providing you a speedy trial—again, immediate grounds for dismissal by a judge. If the court does not provide requested discovery, you can ask to have the case dismissed in court due to being denied evidence you need for your defense. If you choose to ask for discovery, the information you request should include the following:

- **notes made about the stop by the cop**
- **calibration records for the speed measurement device**
- **training records for the cop on that particular speed measurement device**
- **operator manuals and department regulations for use of the speed measurement device**
- **maintenance records for the speed measurement device**
- **studies or documents showing the need for the traffic control method you purportedly violated; engineering reports or research that show rationale for the speed limit**
- **the cop's tickets written that day or month**
- **the department's tickets written that month**

You should carefully review the notes the cop made during the stop for accuracy. For example, if the ticket shows that your bike is blue, and your bike is actually green, it creates room for the argument that the cop stopped the wrong motorcyclist by mistake. If the cop's estimation of the environment (weather, traffic, visibility, signs, signals, and markings) is different from reality, it opens the door to demonstrate that he or she does not remember correctly the circumstances and reason for the stop. If there are very few notes made by the cop or they are clearly inaccurate, this opens the door to discrediting the officer's testimony on the stand by asking questions he or she can't possibly remember. Enough "I don't knows" or "I can't recalls" and you stand a good chance of casting reasonable doubt of the accuracy of the officer's judgment of your driving behavior—whether you broke the law or not. And remember: unlike most amateur PowerPoint presentations, the officer can't just stand there and read the information to you. He or she has to testify from memory, otherwise known as independent recollection. You're not fighting the piece of paper with the citation information on it—you are fighting the state's witness and his or her interpretation of what they saw that day.

Avoid trying to take on a speed measurement device unless it's your only angle possible. However, learning, using, and maintaining a radar unit is a daily ongoing process, and it may be worth learning this information to see if there's any way to cast doubt on the device's accuracy or the cop's skill and qualifications to wield it. Plus, radar shows only the speed of a vehicle; it does not identify the object or the location of the vehicle traveling at that speed. This is where training and calibration come into play. A laser, however, is a targeted tool that is much more accurate and difficult to fight in court. Combine either of these with a visual estimate—relying on the cop's training, experience, and judgment after years of traffic enforcement—is a very difficult combination to beat. Lots of people have beaten a radar ticket successfully, but most everyone who tries, fails.

LEGAL BRIEFS: Enough "I don't knows" or "I can't recalls" from the officer and you stand a good chance of casting reasonable doubt of the accuracy of the officer's judgment of your driving behavior—whether you broke the law or not.

It's also worthwhile to take a look at the engineering studies as well as the police officer's/department's recent traffic citation history. Again, you're looking for that tiny clue, that one variable, which can help you cast doubt on the efficacy of the charge against you. Maybe your bike is a red sport-tourer. What conclusion would you draw if you learned that the same officer wrote similar tickets to four red sport bikes that day? Or, maybe you notice that there was a flurry of ticket-writing activity by the department, all at the same location, and all in the last few days of the calendar month? You might decide to look closer at the location—was there a visual obstruction like a construction vehicle planted there? Did the untrimmed roadside trees make for a slam-dunk speed trap? Did the county recently change the speed limit or signage improperly? Look closely enough at the evidence and something will pop out at you, something you can use either to prove your innocence or at least cast reasonable doubt upon your guilt.

COURTROOM STRATEGY

Once you have your evidence organized and you've identified the weak spots in the prosecutor's case, it's time to plan your defense. Outline your battle plan for getting your ticket dismissed and move from simple to complex as you go. For example, the first (simplest) way to get your ticket dismissed is to try one last time for a Level Two solution: strike a plea bargain with the prosecutor before anyone has to go before the judge. Another simple dismissal is if the police officer does not show up for the trial. No witness, no conviction. You can't cross-examine a piece of paper; you can't confront your accuser if it's a machine like a radar gun. If you were issued a ticket by multiple officers, such as one working a radar on an overpass and another down the road writing citations, both officers are required to be present as witnesses against you. One cannot testify for the other—this is known as hearsay and should not be allowed as evidence. You can ask in either case to have the charge dismissed due to insufficient evidence.

More complex ways to get your ticket dismissed are citing insufficient evidence or inadequate procedures. Remember, you pored over the facts of your case and the exact language of the law under which you were cited. When the prosecution fails to prove one of the necessary points required for a guilty conviction, it's your job to note it (quietly!) and bring it up when the defense rests its case. Maybe the state never proved that you were the person actually driving the vehicle in question; maybe the state never demonstrated that you didn't actually come to a complete stop. Now is the time to pipe up and say, "Whoa, wait a minute! For me to be guilty of A, doesn't the state have to prove I committed W, X, Y, and Z?" Similarly, asking for a dismissal due to poor procedure on the officer's part, particularly in their use of a speed measurement device, is a matter of pointing out that the state/county/department has established rules for the calibration, use, and maintenance of equipment and the officer clearly did not follow procedures B and C.

The worst way to get your charge dismissed is due to an incompetent witness, but it's your right to say so if it's the case. Judges and prosecutors won't be

LEGAL BRIEFS: **More complex ways to get your ticket dismissed are citing insufficient evidence or inadequate procedures.**

happy with you questioning the cop's ability to do his or her job, and they don't often side with the defense even if the defense is correct. But this is the purpose of all the unanswerable questions you asked the officer on the stand. When the judge hears enough "I don't remembers" and "I can't says" you've done a good job of demonstrating that the officer cannot recollect what happened during your stop or that he or she made a mistake that ended up with you getting the citation and not the person who earned it. It ain't pretty, but it's worth a shot.

GOING IN

Rehearse, prepare, have contingency plans ready, and go observe the court process. Get a feel for how things flow, the prosecutor's approach, and become familiar with the process so you don't stumble over your own feet when it's your turn. On the day of your trial, show up early and watch the proceedings carefully. If the judge is clearly grumpy that day and it looks like your hopes are dashed before you even step up to the plate, leave quietly and reschedule your trial. You might get a different judge the next time, or the same judge might be in a more forgiving mood. Also, it's always possible that the cop won't show up. Note: Try this only once. Continually scheduling trials, not showing up, and rescheduling will frustrate the court, and the person who'll lose out is you.

Steps to take if you are forced to enter Level Three—tellin' it to da judge:

- **Try to talk to the prosecutor if you haven't already.**
- **If the prosecutor doesn't offer you a continuance, plead "not guilty." Pleading no contest or guilty by reason of whatever is still guilty in a courtroom.**
- **Hope that the cop doesn't show. If the cop isn't there, the state has no witness, and you're legally in the right to demand that you confront your accuser.**
- **Try to schedule the latest possible court date so the officer has less of a chance of remembering the stop and your interaction. The prosecution's witness, the cop, can't sit there and read from his notes what you**

LEGAL BRIEFS: **If the prosecutor doesn't offer you a continuance, plead "not guilty." Pleading no contest or guilty by reason of whatever is still guilty in a courtroom.**

did or did not say. He has to be able to describe your actions in detail in his own words.

- Try to schedule your court date adjacent to or near a national holiday, if possible (Halloween, Thanksgiving, New Year's Day, Saint Patrick's Day, Memorial Day, Independence Day, and Labor Day are good candidates), as it ups the odds of the officer being either on vacation or on enforcement-saturation patrol duty. Try an Internet or Facebook search of the officer to see if you can find out when his or her birthday is—or better yet, his or her wedding anniversary, ha-ha! You may not have any choice of when your court date is, but you have to try to tip the odds in your favor.
- If you feel the judge is grumpy on that particular day, slip out the back door and reschedule (once).
- Respect the players and the process. Don't waste anyone's time with meaningless bellyaching. Dress nicely (business casual), but not too nicely. (Fancy suits worked for John Gotti, but you ain't John Gotti.)
- Know when the opposition is misusing evidence or testimony against you. (Objections.)
- Make notes of the decision of the judge and ask for clarification if necessary. Comply with all requirements of the decision. Check your driving record after everything's over to make sure it is accurate.
- Don't bother with a lawyer unless you're forced into a guilty verdict and want to appeal it. If you have plenty of money, hire a lawyer right away. The attorney surely would have better luck getting your ticket dismissed before a court trial than you would, and he or she surely would have better luck beating it if it came to trial.

GOOD RESOURCES

National Motorists Association: www.motorists.org

Article: www.worldlawdirect.com/article/903/fighting-speeding-ticket.html

General Information: www.trafficticketsecrets.com

PART

State-by-State Guide to Motorcycle Laws

The next section of the book is a quick and handy reference guide to the various rules and regulations one might encounter while crossing state lines on a cross-country tour. Starting off each section is each state's rideability rank as it compares with the other 50 states and Washington D.C.

State rideability rankings are based on three criteria; population density, law enforcement density, and the ratio of multi-vehicle motorcycle fatalities to single-vehicle motorcycle fatalities (a high ratio, such as 75/25, is bad, as it shows that in a fatal accident in that state, it is more likely that the rider got hit by another vehicle rather than simply having an accident on his or her own). The multi-vehicle to single-vehicle motorcycle crash ratio is a reflection of the combination of local attitude, motorist awareness, population density, and traffic patterns and exposure.

These three statistics however, are not weighted equally in the final tally for the rideability rank. The author surveyed riders as to which of these three indexes were most important to them as it pertains to ranking states for safety and the likelihood of getting through without a ticket, and it was determined that riders were primarily concerned about the fatal crash ratio, followed by population density and lastly, law enforcement density.

It should be noted again that the rideabilty rating you see listed with each state has nothing to do with the number of scenic roads, road conditions, fun destinations, etc., but is only based on safety considerations and law enforcement pressure.

ALABAMA

RIDEABILITY RANK: 28

With a higher ranking being best for motorcyclists, Alabama ranks 25th in the nation for population density and 29th for law enforcement density. Alabama is a state with rolling hills, gentle planes, and seashore. The ratio of multi-vehicle motorcycle fatalities to single-vehicle motorcycle fatalities is 55/45. The typical patrol vehicle is a Ford Police Interceptor (Crown Vic). The overall tone of law enforcement toward motorcycle riders is best described as businesslike.

ALABAMA LAWS IN DETAIL

Alabama uses a demerit points system to track moving violations. Racking up 12 to 14 points in a two-year period gets you a 60-day suspension, 15 to 17 in a two-year period gets you 90 days, 18 to 20 gets you 120 days, 21 to 23 gets you 180 days, and 24 or more points in two years will get you a one-year suspension. With three reckless driving convictions in 12 months, your license will be revoked.

ALABAMA AT A GLANCE

Helmet Law	Yes	Exhaust Noise	No
Eye Protection	Not required	Earphones	Okay
Permit Restrictions	None	Checkpoints	Yes
Insurance	20/40/10	Automated Enforcement	Red light cameras
Reciprocity	Yes	School Buses	Yes
Handlebar Height Restriction	Yes	Pedestrians	Yes
Daytime Headlight Use	Not required	Move-Over Law	Yes
Left Lane Restriction	None	Excessive Speed Sanctions	No
Unchanging Traffic Signal Law	None	Mandatory Tow	No
Turn Signals	Not Required	Feet Down	No
License Plate Display	No	Erratics	None
Fenders	No		

For more detailed information on the above, see next page or reference Chapter 2: U.S. Motorcycle Laws and Regulations.

Speeding 1–25 mph over the posted limit will earn you two points. Speeding 26 or more over will earn you five. Traveling at any rate of speed above 85 is worth five, no matter what the speed limit is. Reckless earns you six. Most other infractions are two to three points, with some of the more serious ones (DWI, passing a school bus, failure to yield) upwards of five or six points. Points drop off your record after two years, but the conviction remains on your record.

HELMET LAW: All riders and passengers are required to wear motorcycle helmets.
HANDLEBAR HEIGHT RESTRICTION: Handlebars may rise to no more than 15 inches above the operator's seat.
EQUIPMENT REQUIREMENTS: A passenger seat and footrests are required if the rider is carrying a passenger, and at least one rearview mirror is required.

GOOD RESOURCES
Alabama Department of Public Safety: http://dps.alabama.gov
Alabama Statutes: http://www.legislature.state.al.us

ALASKA

RIDEABILITY RANK: 13

With a higher ranking being best for motorcyclists, Alaska ranks first in the nation for population density and 17th for law enforcement density. Alaska is a challenging, scenic, adventure-filled state. Roadways tend to be rough and scenic, and wildlife sightings are frequent and dangerous. The ratio of multi-vehicle motorcycle fatalities to single-vehicle motorcycle fatalities is 56/44.The typical patrol vehicle is a Ford Police Interceptor (Crown Vic) or Ford Expedition. The overall tone of law enforcement toward motorcycle riders is best described as businesslike.

ALASKA LAWS IN DETAIL

Alaska uses a demerit points system for moving violations, and suspensions and revocations are mandatory. If you run up 12 points in 12 months or 18 points in 24 months, expect a suspension or revocation. Major infractions (such as fleeing, racing, or reckless) max out at 10 points. Speeding less than 10 over is two points, 10–19 is four points, and 20 or more is worth six points. You can earn "credit" for citation-free

ALASKA AT A GLANCE

Helmet Law	Partial	Exhaust Noise	No
Eye Protection	Yes	Earphones	Prohibited by law
Permit Restrictions	Yes	Checkpoints	No
Insurance	50/100/25	Automated Enforcement	Yes
Reciprocity	Yes	School Buses	Yes
Handlebar Height Restriction	Yes	Pedestrians	Yes
Daytime Headlight Use	No	Move-Over Law	Yes
Left Lane Restriction	No	Excessive Speed Sanctions	No
Unchanging Traffic Signal Law	No	Mandatory Tow	No
Turn Signals	Required by law	Feet Down	No
License Plate Display	Yes	Erratics	Yes
Fenders	Required by law		

For more detailed information on the above, see next page or reference Chapter 2: U.S. Motorcycle Laws and Regulations.

driving and/or participating in a driver improvement clinic. This can be done once per year for credit.

Alaska is not a member of the Nonresident Violator Compact (NRVC), which is meant to ensure equal treatment of nonresidents and residents and to standardize methods for processing citations, as well as the response of the rider/driver to comply to them. This means that if you're nabbed for a moving violation here, the arresting officer is not obligated to release you without posting bond for the fine. If you don't have a method of posting bond (cash works; checks and credit may work), you could end up in jail until you do. And, if you are required to pay the fine or appear in court and fail to do so, your home state will not necessarily suspend your license until you comply with the citation's requirements (pay the fine). The state might never even know about it. States that are not members of this compact are Alaska, California, Michigan, Montana, Oregon, and Wisconsin.

HELMET LAW: Riders under 18 and all passengers regardless of age are required to wear helmets that meet or exceed DOT standards.

EYE PROTECTION: Eye protection is required unless your bike has a windshield with a height of 15 inches or greater above the handlebars.

PERMIT RESTRICTIONS: A DOT helmet is required. A rider on a permit must also be under the direct supervision of a licensed rider 21 or older who has held a motorcycle license for a year or more.

TURN SIGNALS: Required by law if original equipment.

LICENSE PLATE DISPLAY: Illuminated if originally equipped. No covers are allowed.

EQUIPMENT REQUIREMENTS: Motorcycles are required to have two mirrors, left and right; fenders on both wheels; and a passenger seat, footrests, and handholds if carrying a passenger. They may be required to pass a random inspection.

ERRATICS: State law requires you to keep both hands on the handlebars.

GOOD RESOURCES
Alaska Laws: www.legis.state.ak.us
Alaska Division of Motor Vehicles: http://doa.alaska.gov/dmv

ARIZONA

RIDEABILITY RANK: 27

With a higher ranking being best for motorcyclists, Arizona ranks 19th in the nation for population density and 21st for law enforcement density. Arizona is a desert state with lonely highways, national forests, and rugged mountains. Roadways tend to be perfect for motorcycling—clean and well maintained. The ratio of multi-vehicle motorcycle fatalities to single-vehicle motorcycle fatalities is 63/37. The typical patrol vehicle is a Ford Police Interceptor (Crown Vic), Charger, or SUV. The overall tone of law enforcement toward motorcycle riders is best described as businesslike.

ARIZONA LAWS IN DETAIL

Arizona uses a demerit points system to track moving violations. Individuals who accumulate eight to 12 points in a year may be required to attend a driver improvement clinic. (Running a red light makes this driver's education course mandatory.) Speeding tickets are worth three points each. Two or more convictions for

ARIZONA AT A GLANCE

Helmet Law	**Partial**	Exhaust Noise	**No**
Eye Protection	**Required by law**	Earphones	**Okay**
Permit Restrictions	**Yes**	Checkpoints	**Yes**
Insurance	**15/30/10**	Automated Enforcement	**No**
Reciprocity	**Yes**	School Buses	**Yes**
Handlebar Height Restriction	**Yes**	Pedestrians	**Yes**
Daytime Headlight Use	**No**	Move-Over Law	**Yes**
Left Lane Restriction	**No**	Excessive Speed Sanctions	**Yes**
Unchanging Traffic Signal Law	**No**	Mandatory Tow	**No**
Turn Signals	**Not Required**	HOV	**Okay**
License Plate Display	**Yes**	Feet Down	**No**
Fenders	**Not Required**	Erratics	**Yes**

For more detailed information on the above, see next page or reference Chapter 2: U.S. Motorcycle Laws and Regulations.

reckless driving and racing (eight points each) will get you revoked. Convictions remain on your record for five years.

HELMET LAW: Partial. Only riders under 18 are required to wear helmets.

EYE PROTECTION: Riders are required to wear glasses, goggles, or a face shield unless the bike is equipped with a windshield.

PERMIT RESTRICTIONS: Riders on a motorcycle permit are prohibited from carrying passengers or riding on freeways or interstate highways. Permit holders may also not ride at night or during low visibility (visibility reduced to less than 500 feet).

HANDLEBAR HEIGHT RESTRICTION: Handlebars cannot rise above the operator's seated shoulder height.

UNCHANGING TRAFFIC SIGNAL LAW: It should be noted that running red lights in built-up areas of Arizona is a sore spot with law enforcement—and there is no accommodation for riders stuck at an unchanging traffic signal.

LICENSE PLATE DISPLAY: Any frame, holder, or cover that prevents the plate from being clearly legible is prohibited. State law even goes so far as to point out that the word *Arizona* (or wherever you live, presumably) at the top of the plate cannot be covered.

EXCESSIVE SPEED SANCTIONS: Traveling more than 35 mph approaching a school crossing, 20 over in a business or residential district (or over 45 if no speed is posted), and 86 mph and over is considered excessive speed with increased penalties—up to 30 days in jail and $500.

EQUIPMENT REQUIREMENTS: At least one rearview mirror is required. A passenger seat, footrests, and handholds are required if you're carrying a passenger, and an annual inspection is required.

ERRATICS: A speeding ticket of 65 mph or less on a 55-mph road is a minor infraction. It is considered a "waste of a finite resource" (fossil fuels, presumably) that doesn't count toward license suspension.

GOOD RESOURCES
Arizona Motor Vehicle Division: www.azdot.gov/mvd
Arizona Revised Statutes: www.azleg.gov

ARKANSAS

RIDEABILITY RANK: 17

With a higher ranking being best for motorcyclists, Arkansas ranks 18th in the nation for population density and 25th for law enforcement density. Arkansas is a surprisingly mountainous state with fertile delta and prairie lands. Roadways tend to be well paved, with lots marked "crooked and steep." The ratio of multi-vehicle motorcycle fatalities to single-vehicle motorcycle fatalities is 52/48.The typical patrol vehicle is a Ford Police Interceptor (Crown Vic), Dodge Charger, or Chevy Impala. The overall tone of law enforcement toward motorcycle riders is best described as businesslike.

ARKASAS AT A GLANCE

Helmet Law	Partial	Exhaust Noise	No
Eye Protection	Required by law	Earphones	Okay
Permit Restrictions	None	Checkpoints	Yes
Insurance	25/50/15	Automated Enforcement	No
Reciprocity	Yes	School Buses	Yes
Handlebar Height Restriction	None	Pedestrians	Yes
Daytime Headlight Use	Required by law	Move-Over Law	Yes
Left Lane Restriction	None	Excessive Speed Sanctions	Yes
Unchanging Traffic Signal Law	Yes	Mandatory Tow	No
Turn Signals	Not Required	Feet Down	No
License Plate Display	No	Erratics	Yes
Fenders	Not required		

For more detailed information on the above, see next page or reference Chapter 2: U.S. Motorcycle Laws and Regulations.

ARKANSAS LAWS IN DETAIL

Arkansas uses a demerit points system to monitor traffic violations. Reaching 14 to 17 points may get you a suspension of up to three months; 18 to 23 points is a six-month suspension; and 24-plus means you're suspended for a year. However, each of these suspension thresholds also involves an administrative hearing, and the hearing officer can use discretion when meting out retribution for problem driving behavior. Failing to attend a hearing just means an automatic suspension.

Speeding up to 10 mph over the limit is worth three points. Traveling 11–20 over is worth four points, 21–30 over is worth five, and 30 or greater over the limit will get you eight points. It is also important to note that in Arkansas, three violations within 12 months draws the attention of the local licensing authority.

HELMET LAW: Riders under 21 are required to wear helmets that conform to FVMSS 218.

EYE PROTECTION: Riders must wear glasses, goggles, or a face shield.

UNCHANGING TRAFFIC SIGNAL LAW: Referring only for those traffic lights that use a sensor to detect vehicles, you can proceed through an unchanging red light if the traffic light does not detect your motorcycle as long as you come to a complete stop, exercise due care, and proceed with caution when safe. Sweet.

EXCESSIVE SPEED SANCTIONS: Anything more than 15 over the limit is considered excessive speeding and can get you up to 30 days in jail and increased fines.

EQUIPMENT REQUIREMENTS: Motorcycles must have at least one rearview mirror and—if you're carrying a passenger—a passenger seat, footrests, and handholds.

ERRATICS: Riders under 16 may not carry passengers. Children younger than eight are not allowed to ride as passengers.

GOOD RESOURCES

Arkansas Office of Driver Services: www.dfa.arkansas.gov
Arkansas State Laws: www.arkleg.state.ar.us

CALIFORNIA

RIDEABILITY RANK: 35

With a higher ranking being best for motorcyclists, California ranks 40th in the nation for population density and 15th for law enforcement density. The California riding environment varies widely depending on elevation and proximity to the coast. Mountain roadways tend to be tight and twisty. Coastal roadways tend to be moderately twisty, wide, and scenic. Central Valley and desert roads tend to be straight and dull. The ratio of multi-vehicle motorcycle fatalities to single-vehicle motorcycle fatalities is 61/39. California is known informally as notorious for writing traffic tickets. The typical patrol vehicle is a Ford Police Interceptor (Crown Vic) or Dodge Charger. Police also use Harley-Davidson, Honda, and BMW motorcycles. The overall tone of law enforcement toward motorcycle riders is best described as businesslike tending toward enthusiastic. A rash of crashes or a large event in the area can quickly ramp local law enforcement's tone up to aggressive.

CALIFORNIA AT A GLANCE

Helmet Law	Yes	Exhaust Noise	Yikes (see next page)
Eye Protection	Not required		
Permit Restrictions	Yes	Earphones	One ear only
Insurance	15/30/5	Checkpoints	Yes
Reciprocity	Yes	Automated Enforcement	Red light cameras; rail crossings
Handlebar Height Restriction	Yes	School Buses	Yes
Daytime Headlight Use	Required by law	Pedestrians	Yes
Left Lane Restriction	Unfortunately Not	Move-Over Law	Yes
Unchanging Traffic Signal Law	No	Excessive Speed Sanctions	Yes
Turn Signals	Required by law	Mandatory Tow	Yes
License Plate Display	Yes	HOV	Okay
Fenders	Not required	Feet Down	Not required
		Erratics	Yes

For more detailed information on the above, see next page or reference Chapter 2: U.S. Motorcycle Laws and Regulations.

CALIFORNIA LAWS IN DETAIL

California uses a points system for driving records. Minor infractions such as an at-fault accident or moving violation will cost you one point. More serious infractions such as reckless, hit-and-run, driving after suspension, and DUI will cost you two points. If you accumulate four points in 12 months, six points in 24 months, or eight points in 36 months, the state can suspend or revoke your license.

Speeding tickets in California are not cheap. Expect to pay upwards of $350, including penalties and assessments. And contrary to popular belief, driving records are not automatically cleared of all points once the points are over a year old.

California is not a member of the Nonresident Violator Compact (NRVC), which is meant to ensure equal treatment of nonresidents and residents and to standardize methods for processing citations, as well as the response of the rider/driver to comply to them. This means that if you're nabbed for a moving violation here, the arresting officer is not obligated to release you without posting bond for the fine. If you don't have a method of posting bond (cash works; checks and credit may work), you could end up in jail until you do. And, if you are required to pay the fine or appear in court and fail to do so, your home state will not necessarily suspend your license until you comply with the citation's requirements (pay the fine). Your home state may never even know about it. States that are not members of this compact are Alaska, California, Michigan, Montana, Oregon, and Wisconsin.

HELMET LAW: DOT-compliant helmets are required for all riders and passengers.
PERMIT RESTRICTIONS: The operator cannot carry passengers, ride on freeways, or ride at night.
HANDLEBARS: Handlebars can rise no more than 6 inches above the operator's seated shoulder height.
DAYTIME HEADLIGHT USE: Required by law except for bikes older than 1978.
TURN SIGNALS: Electric signals are required by law for all bikes 1973 and newer.
LICENSE PLATE: Plates must be displayed rearward, securely fastened, clearly visible, and clearly legible. The license plate must also be at least 12 inches but not more than 60 inches from the ground. Plates must be clearly visible up to 50 feet behind the vehicle.
EXHAUST NOISE: The Motorcycle Anti-Tampering Act goes into effect in 2013. All motorcycles are required to have either stock or aftermarket exhaust with an EPA stamp. The stamp must certify compliance with emissions regulations and that the pipe does not exceed 80 decibels. Citations will carry fines from $100 to $250. Current state law emphasizes that mufflers need to prevent excessive or unusual noise, and it prohibits modifications such as a cutout, bypass, whistle tip, or similar. Decibel level limits are 80 (1986 and newer) to 92 (older than 1970) with different requirements in between, depending on the year of your bike.
EARPHONES: Headphones and earphones may be used in one ear only. There are no requirements for helmet speakers, but headphones and earphones that cover or insert into the ears cannot be used in both ears.

CHECKPOINTS: Most are to test cars for working smog components and CARB certifications.

AUTOMATED ENFORCEMENT: Red light cameras are in use, and some toll roads time drivers between tolls to ensure speed limit compliance.

SCHOOL BUSES: When a school bus is stopped and displaying flashing red lights and a stop arm, you must stop before passing the bus from either direction. This law does not apply to divided highways or multiple-lane highways when the bus is on the other side of the road. A bus driver who witnesses you passing illegally can report you to the police up to 24 hours later.

PEDESTRIANS: Drivers must yield right of way to pedestrians crossing at an intersection in a marked or an unmarked crosswalk. Pedestrians are required to obey crossing signals and yield right of way to vehicles already legally within an intersection. If a vehicle is stopped for the purpose of yielding the right of way to pedestrians in an intersection, you can't pass that vehicle.

MOVE-OVER LAW: On a freeway (generally, any controlled-access highway) when passing a parked emergency vehicle with lights flashing, including tow trucks or DOT vehicles, you are required either to move over to the next lane or, if you can't do so, slow down.

EXCESSIVE SPEED SANCTIONS: A hundred miles an hour or more can cost you up to $500 and get your license suspended for 30 days for a first offense. A second offense within three years can cost you up to $750 and another suspension. Three within five years goes up to $1,000. Speed contests (whether racing against another rider or a stopwatch) are not tolerated and lead to hefty fines, jail time, community service, and a three- to six-month suspension for a first offense. A second offense within five years is double trouble. If you injure somebody, you're screwed. And don't even think about fleeing or evading.

MANDATORY TOW: If you're stopped and you don't have a proper license for the vehicle you're driving, the state is technically required to tow your vehicle. However, reports suggest that this is not consistently enforced statewide, and police officers still use their judgment when deciding whether or not to tow.

EQUIPMENT REQUIREMENTS: Bikes are required to have at least one rearview mirror as well as a passenger seat and footrests if you are carrying a passenger. Electric turn signals are required for bikes 1973 and newer. Bikes are required to have at least one red rearward-facing reflector. Motorcycle equipment inspections are random. Batteries are required to have enough power to light the taillight for 15 minutes without engine power. Bikes 1966 or newer must have brakes on both front and rear wheels (older bikes can have a brake on only one wheel), and there are requirements for brakes' effectiveness/stopping distance.

ERRATICS: California is the only state in the country that allows lane splitting, lane sharing, and filtering. However, contrary to legend, lane splitting is not legal. Nor is it illegal. It falls into a gray area unique to California. Overall, law enforcement accepts lane splitting and doesn't view it as a safety hazard, particularly in Southern California. This means that splitting lanes is tolerated because of its subtle benefits to traffic congestion and California's motorcycle-heavy culture. But bear in mind:

You can (and will) get stopped and cited if you're riding like an ass. You can get a ticket for unsafe speed, unsafe lane change, or lane "straddling" while splitting lanes if the police officer views your behavior as dangerous or unnecessary.

LANE SPLITTING GUIDELINES: Splitting lanes, above all else, must be done in a safe and prudent manner. Big, fat bikes are not adept at lane splitting, so if your ride of choice is a big tourer or dresser, think twice. Also, this is not a technique for beginners! You want years of experience with heavy, congested traffic—to the point where other drivers' harebrained maneuvers never really surprise you anymore. If you've got fewer than 10 years driving experience and five years' motorcycle experience, I advise against lane splitting. A vehicle's sudden lane change, opened door, or an arm—or leg!—draped out a window could lead to injury or worse.

Lane splitting is a way to reduce congestion and keep your engine from overheating—it's not a right or even a privilege. Consider it a tool for managing slow, heavy traffic. You should split lanes only when traffic is moving less than 30 mph—ideally, only when traffic is moving slower than 5 mph—and keep your speed to no more than 10 mph over that of the prevailing traffic. It is said to be safest to split the number 1 and 2 lanes (left/fast lane and the one next to it) and try to remain within one of those lanes wherever possible; weaving back and forth between 1 and 2 can get you a ticket. Keep your attention focused at least 150 feet ahead of you to observe openings in traffic that prompt other vehicles to change lanes. I'd recommend watching for turn signals, but everybody knows that no one in California uses them anyway.

SEAT HEIGHT: The law states that you have to be able to reach the ground with both feet while seated.

GOOD RESOURCES
California Motorcycle Manual: http://www.dmv.ca.gov/portal/home/dmv.htm
California Vehicle Code: http://www.dmv.ca.gov/pubs/vctop/vc/vc.htm

COLORADO

RIDEABILITY RANK: 22

With a higher ranking being best for motorcyclists, Colorado ranks 15th in the nation for population density and 30th for law enforcement density. Colorado is a rugged Rocky Mountain, high-plains, and high-desert state. Roadways tend to be scenic and well maintained. The ratio of multi-vehicle motorcycle fatalities to single-vehicle motorcycle fatalities is 55/45. The typical patrol vehicle is a Ford Police Interceptor (Crown Vic), Charger, or SUV. The overall tone of law enforcement toward motorcycle riders is best described as businesslike.

COLORADO LAWS IN DETAIL

Colorado uses a points system to track moving violations. Convictions remain on your record for seven years. Adult drivers 21 or older will have their license suspended for up to a year for racking up 12 points in a year or 18 points in two years. Minors 18 to 20 will have their licenses suspended for nine points in a year or 12 points in two years—or for accumulating 14 points between the ages of 18 and 21. Riders under

COLORADO AT A GLANCE

Helmet Law	Partial	Exhaust Noise	Oh, yeah
Eye Protection	Required by law	Earphones	Prohibited by law
Permit Restrictions	Yes	Checkpoints	Yes
Insurance	25/50/15, No-fault	Automated Enforcement	Yes
		School Buses	Yes
Reciprocity	Yes	Pedestrians	Yes
Handlebar Height Restriction	No	Move-Over Law	Yes
Daytime Headlight Use	Not required	Excessive Speed Sanctions	No
Left Lane Restriction	Yes	Mandatory Tow	No
Unchanging Traffic Signal Law	None	HOV	Okay
Turn Signals	Not required	Feet Down	No
License Plate Display	No	Erratics	Yes
Fenders	Not required		

For more detailed information on the above, see next page or reference Chapter 2: U.S. Motorcycle Laws and Regulations.

18 will get suspended for six points in 12 months or for having seven or more points accrue before their 18th birthday.

Speeding tickets for less than 10 mph over the limit cost you one point. From 10–19, they'll cost you four; 20–39 will get you six; 40 mph or over earns you 12. Reckless is worth eight, and most other minor infractions are two to four points. When DMV officials plan to suspend your license, they'll send you a notice and schedule a hearing to determine whether the suspension is valid and for how long; the hearing officer has some discretion there. If you skip the hearing, you'll be suspended for the maximum: one year.

Three or more convictions for reckless riding in seven years makes you a habitual offender. After that, the habitual offender law gets complicated. However, it more or less states that 10 or more convictions of four or more points in five years—or 18 or more convictions of one to three points in five years—will likely lead to your license being revoked.

HELMET LAW: Riders younger than 18 are required to wear helmets that meet FMVSS 218 specifications.

EYE PROTECTION: Eye protection for both operators and passengers is required by law: glasses, goggles, or a face shield. Windshields don't count.

PERMIT RESTRICTIONS: Riders operating under an instruction permit may do so only while under the immediate supervision of a licensed Colorado motorcyclist 21 or older. If you're under 18, it must be your parent or guardian or a person formally designated by them.

LEFT LANE RESTRICTION: On 65-mph or greater roads, the only reasons you can be in the left lane is if it's an HOV lane, if you're passing, or if you're turning. In the case of an HOV lane on a three-lane freeway, the middle lane becomes the left lane/passing lane.

EXHAUST NOISE: The state of Colorado doesn't do much different than most other states when it comes to motorcycle noise, but the city of Denver does. See "Erratics" below.

EARPHONES: The use of headphones or earphones is prohibited by law, although speakers mounted inside a helmet are considered okay.

HOV: Motorcycles are permitted to use HOV lanes unless specifically marked as prohibited.

EQUIPMENT REQUIREMENTS: At least one rearview mirror is required, and a passenger seat and footrests are required if carrying a passenger. A random inspection, including emissions, may be required in some areas.

ERRATICS: Colorado has become known for strict exhaust regulations, thanks to the citizens of Denver. All motorcycles within the Denver city limits are required to have an EPA label, retroactive back to 1982 (when the EPA first noticed motorcycles existed). This effectively means that aftermarket pipes, no matter how quiet or good at reducing emissions, are illegal if they don't have an EPA stamp. A conviction can cost you $500.

Due to some of the extreme grades in Colorado, there is a special law regarding Interstate 70. When there's on an uphill grade of 6 percent or more for at least a mile, you can't use the far-left lane at a speed of less than the minimum or 10 less than the maximum, whichever is lower. So if you're chugging along at 34 mph in the left lane and the minimum is 45 and the maximum is 65, there'd better be a good reason.

Because of some of the extreme grades in Colorado, coasting is prohibited. This is not unusual for states (most states cite somewhere that coasting is prohibited), but law enforcement officials look at it a lot more closely in mountain states because it represents an additional safety hazard. "How will they know?" you ask yourself. The same way you know whether you're in gear or not: The bike sounds different, it's usually quieter, and there are ways to observe the action of the clutch and throttle while listening to the engine that are a dead giveaway. The lesson here is to keep your bike in gear with the clutch lever released when heading down a steep grade.

GOOD RESOURCES

Colorado Division of Motor Vehicles: www.colorado.gov/revenue/dmv
Colorado State Statutes: www.state.co.us

CONNECTICUT

RIDEABILITY RANK: 39

With a higher ranking being best for motorcyclists, Connecticut ranks 47th in the nation for population density and 24th for law enforcement density. Connecticut is a historic state with rolling hills, rivers, and covered bridges. Roadways tend to be busy. The ratio of multi-vehicle motorcycle fatalities to single-vehicle motorcycle fatalities is 57/43. Connecticut is known informally as a state notorious for writing traffic tickets. The typical patrol vehicle is a Ford Police Interceptor (Crown Vic). The overall tone of law enforcement toward motorcycle riders is best described as businesslike.

CONNECTICUT LAWS IN DETAIL

Connecticut uses a demerit points system to track moving violations. Speeding tickets cost you one point. More egregious violations run you two to four points. Points remain on your record for two years. When you reach 11 points, the DMV will suspend your license for 30 days. Every time you go over 10 points again within five years of a

CONNECTICUT AT A GLANCE

Helmet Law	Partial under 18	Exhaust Noise	Yes
Eye Protection	Required by law	Earphones	Okay
Permit Restrictions	Yes	Checkpoints	Yes
Insurance	20/40/10	Automated Enforcement	No
Reciprocity	Yes	School Buses	Yes
Handlebar Height Restriction	Yes	Pedestrians	Yes
Daytime Headlight Use	Required by law	Move-Over Law	Yes
Left Lane Restriction	None	Excessive Speed Sanctions	Yes
Unchanging Traffic Signal Law	No	Mandatory Tow	No
Turn Signals	Required by law	HOV	Okay
License Plate Display	No	Feet Down	No
Fenders	Required by law	Erratics	Yes

For more detailed information on the above, see next page or reference Chapter 2: U.S. Motorcycle Laws and Regulations.

suspension, your license will be suspended until you drop back down to 10 points. Sounds manageable, right?

The problem is that there are limits to the number of speeding tickets you can get. Once you hit four within two years, expect to get your license suspended for 30 days for a fourth violation, 60 days for a fifth violation, and six months for each subsequent violation.

Getting nicked for "excessive speeding," defined as 15 mph or above the limit, can bump your total fine up by 25 percent. And if you are 24 years old or younger with two moving violation convictions on your record, or 25 or older with three convictions, you'll be required to participate in a driver improvement clinic ("operator retraining program").

HELMET LAW: Riders under 18 are required to wear helmets that meet FMVSS 218 standards.

EYE PROTECTION: Eye protection is required; a windshield or windscreen qualifies as eye protection.

PERMIT RESTRICTIONS: Riders on a permit must wear FMVSS 218–compliant helmets regardless of age and cannot ride on multiple-lane, limited-access highways.

HANDLEBAR HEIGHT RESTRICTION: Handlebars cannot rise above the level of the rider's shoulders when seated.

DAYTIME HEADLIGHT USE: Headlights are required except for bikes older than 1980.

FENDERS: Fenders front and rear are required by law. However, the law also states that if the body of the vehicle or attachments provide adequate protection to limit spray/splash to the rear, it's legal.

EXHAUST NOISE: Connecticut law states that no rider shall use a muffler lacking interior baffle plates or other effective muffling devices, a gutted muffler, or a cutout or straight pipe on the street. The law also prohibits anyone from removing all or part of a muffler, except for repair or replacement for the more effective prevention of noise. To top it off, it's prohibited to use any extension or device that causes excessive or unusual noise.

REQUIRED EQUIPMENT: At least one rearview mirror is required, and fenders are required for both front and rear. A passenger seat and footrests are required if carrying a passenger, and a working odometer is required. The bike must also have one red reflector at the rear, and motorcycles may be subject to a random inspection.

ERRATICS: Riders who have had their endorsements for fewer than three months cannot carry a passenger. Riders 16 or 17 who have not had their endorsements for at least six months cannot carry a passenger.

GOOD RESOURCES
Connecticut Laws Chapter 248: www.cga.ct.gov
Connecticut Department of Motor Vehicles: www.ct.gov/dmv

DELAWARE

RIDEABILITY RANK: 37

With a higher ranking being best for motorcyclists, Delaware ranks 45th in the nation for population density and 28th for law enforcement density. Delaware is a relatively flat, coastal seashore and forest state. Roadways tend to be flat and straight. The ratio of multi-vehicle motorcycle fatalities to single-vehicle motorcycle fatalities is 51/49. The typical patrol vehicle is a Ford Police Interceptor (Crown Vic), with a few Harleys and Dodge Durangos thrown in. The overall tone of law enforcement toward motorcycle riders is best described as businesslike.

DELAWARE LAWS IN DETAIL

Delaware uses a points system to track moving violations. Speeding less than 10 over gets you two points. Speeding 10–14 over gets you four, 15–19 gets you five, and 20 or more gets you five and likely a suspension. A total of 12 points within two years gets you a driver improvement clinic. Accumulating 14 points will get your license

DELAWARE AT A GLANCE

Helmet Law	Partial	Exhaust Noise	No
Eye Protection	Required by law	Earphones	Okay
Permit Restrictions	Yes	Checkpoints	Yes
Insurance	15/30/5	Automated Enforcement	Red light cameras
Reciprocity	Yes	School Buses	Yes
Handlebar Height Restriction	No	Pedestrians	Yes
Daytime Headlight Use	No	Move-Over Law	Yes
Left Lane Restriction	None	Excessive Speed Sanctions	Yes
Unchanging Traffic Signal Law	None	Mandatory Tow	No
Turn Signals	Required by law	Feet Down	No
License Plate Display	Yes	Erratics	Yes
Fenders	Required by law		

For more detailed information on the above, see next page or reference Chapter 2: U.S. Motorcycle Laws and Regulations.

suspended for four months, and the driver improvement program is mandatory. For every two additional points, add two additional months of suspension. Points count fully against you for 12 months, and they are reduced by half during the 12- to 24-month period. Points drop off after two years.

Getting nicked for 25 mph or more over the limit will get you suspended for a month, and you'll get an additional month for every 5 mph over 25. At 25–29, you can take a driver improvement clinic to stave off your suspension. At 30 mph or over, suspension is mandatory. Fifty over, or 100 mph, will get you suspended for a year. Three reckless convictions in a year will get you revoked.

However, a speeding conviction of 14 mph or less over the limit won't cost you any points if it's the first within three years; you just pay the ticket. You can also take a driver improvement clinic once every three years to remove three points from your record.

HELMET LAW: Riders who are younger than 19 years old are required to wear helmets. Riders 19 or older are required only to have a helmet in their possession. Reflectorization on helmets is also required.

EYE PROTECTION: Protective eyewear is required by law. Riders must wear glasses, goggles, or a helmet face shield. A windshield doesn't cut it.

PERMIT RESTRICTIONS: Riders operating on a motorcycle permit may not carry passengers, ride at night, or ride on an interstate freeway. Permit riders are also required to wear helmets and eye protection.

LICENSE PLATE DISPLAY: Unauthorized frames, accessories, designs, or symbols on or attached to the plate are prohibited.

EQUIPMENT REQUIREMENTS: At least one rearview mirror is required, as are fenders front and rear. A red reflector on the rear is also required. If you carry a passenger, a passenger seat and footrests are required. Turn signals, a speedometer, and an inspection are required too.

ERRATICS: The law requires you to keep at least one hand on the bars at all times while moving.

GOOD RESOURCES
Delaware Division of Motor Vehicles: www.dmv.de.gov
Delaware Code Title 21: http://delcode.delaware.gov

DISTRICT OF COLUMBIA

RIDEABILITY RANK: 50 (TIED WITH NEW JERSEY)

The District of Columbia is tied with New Jersey as the worst in the nation for population density. D.C. also comes in the worst for law enforcement density, tied with Louisiana at 50 . . . though there is really no comparison between the two. Washington D.C. is a tight combination of government buildings, historical sites, and public parks. The ratio of multi-vehicle motorcycle fatalities to single-vehicle motorcycle fatalities is 75/25. The typical patrol vehicle is a Ford Police Interceptor (Crown Vic) or Chevy Impala.

DISTRICT OF COLUMBIA AT A GLANCE

Helmet Law	Yes	Exhaust Noise	No
Eye Protection	Required by law	Earphones	Prohibited
Permit Restrictions	None	Checkpoints	Yes
Insurance	20/40/10	Automated Enforcement	Yes
Reciprocity	Yes	School Buses	Yes
Handlebar Height Restriction	Yes	Pedestrians	Yes
Daytime Headlight Use	Not required.	Move-Over Law	No
Left Lane Restriction	None	Excessive Speed Sanctions	No
Unchanging Traffic Signal Law	No	Mandatory Tow	No
Turn Signals	Required by law	HOV	Okay
License Plate Display	No	Feet Down	No
Fenders	Required by law	Erratics	Yes

For more detailed information on the above, see next page or reference Chapter 2: U.S. Motorcycle Laws and Regulations.

DISTRICT OF COLUMBIA LAWS IN DETAIL

The District of Columbia uses a demerit points system to track moving violations. Speeding 11–15 mph over the limit will get you three points, 16–20 will get you four, 21 or over will get you five. Reckless is an automatic 12.

If you rack up 10 or 11 points, your license will be suspended for 90 days. Twelve or more points gets you revoked for six months. More egregious infractions can get you revoked right away, as well. Points remain on your record for two years. A full year with no moving violation convictions can reduce your point total in some instances.

You can sometimes have points from a conviction removed from your record if you participate in a driver improvement clinic within 30 days. You can also accumulate "safe driving points" by going conviction-free for a calendar year. These points can offset existing or new-point violations, but they expire after five years.

HELMET LAW: Helmets are required for all operators and passengers regardless of age or license status.

EYE PROTECTION: Glasses, goggles, or a face shield is required by law unless the bike has a windscreen.

HANDLEBAR HEIGHT RESTRICTION: Handlebars can rise to no greater than 15 inches above the operator's seat.

EQUIPMENT REQUIREMENTS: At least one rearview mirror is required, and fenders front and rear are required. A passenger seat, footrests, and handholds are required if carrying a passenger, and a working speedometer is required.

ERRATICS: Use or possession of radar detectors is prohibited in the District of Columbia.

GOOD RESOURCES

District of Columbia Department of Motor Vehicles: http://dmv.washingtondc.gov

District of Columbia Laws: www.dcregs.dc.gov

FLORIDA

RIDEABILITY RANK: 47

Down near the bottom in rideability ranking, Florida sits 44th in the nation for population density (higher ranking being best for motorcyclists) and 40th for law enforcement density. Florida is a flat peninsula state with seemingly limitless coastline, beaches, and wetlands. Roadways tend to be flat and straight, with lots of intersections. The ratio of multi-vehicle motorcycle fatalities to single-vehicle motorcycle fatalities is 65/35.The typical patrol vehicle is a Ford Police Interceptor (Crown Vic) or Chevy Impala, with some SUVs, motorcycles, and Chargers. The overall tone of law enforcement toward motorcycle riders is best described as enthusiastic.

FLORIDA LAWS IN DETAIL

Florida uses a demerit points system to track moving violations. If you accumulate 12 points in a year, plan to be suspended for up to 30 days. If you rack up 18 points in 18 months, that will get you up to a three-month suspension. And 24 points in three

FLORIDA AT A GLANCE

Helmet Law	Partial	Exhaust Noise	No
Eye Protection	Required by law	Earphones	Prohibited by law
Permit Restrictions	None	Checkpoints	Yes
Insurance	10/20/10, No-fault	Automated Enforcement	Red light cameras
		School Buses	Yes
Reciprocity	Yes	Pedestrians	Yes
Handlebar Height Restriction	Yes	Move-Over Law	Yes
Daytime Headlight Use	Required by law	Excessive Speed Sanctions	Oh, yeah
Left Lane Restriction	No	Mandatory Tow	No
Unchanging Traffic Signal Law	No	HOV	Okay
Turn Signals	No	Feet Down	No
License Plate Display	Yes	Erratics	Yes
Fenders	No		

For more detailed information on the above, see next page or reference Chapter 2: U.S. Motorcycle Laws and Regulations.

years will get you suspended for up to a year. A speeding ticket up to 15 mph over the limit will cost you three points. A citation of 16 or more or a reckless conviction will get you four points. Any speeding citation that accompanies a crash will get you six points. Ultrasonic speeds will cost you big in fines (see below). Three reckless in a year or racing will get you revoked. Getting 15 moving violations (that qualify for demerit points) in five years can also get you revoked.

HELMET LAW: If you are 21 or older and carry at least $10,000 in medical insurance, you can ride without a helmet. Everyone younger than 16 must wear helmets and can ride only as passengers on motorcycles. Riders and passengers 16 to 20 must wear a helmet. Helmets must meet FMVSS 218 standards.

EYE PROTECTION: Glasses, goggles, or a face shield is required of all motorcycle operators on public roads.

INSURANCE: Though it's recommended, motorcyclists are generally not required to carry liability insurance in Florida. If you're involved in a crash with another vehicle, you are still responsible to pay for damages you caused. After a crash, DWI, etc., a mandatory minimum liability policy will be required.

HANDLEBAR HEIGHT RESTRICTION: Handlebars cannot rise above the level of the operator's shoulders while he or she is seated.

LICENSE PLATE DISPLAY: Plates must be permanently mounted and may not be adjusted or capable of being "flipped up." There have been reports that Florida residents in violation of this code are subject to fines of $1,000 to $2,500, but out-of-state riders are generally okay if they're complying with the mounting requirements of their own state—and that the plate is not an obvious violation or attempt to disguise. It is unlawful to alter the plate or use any device—or apply any substance or covering—that interferes with legibility or visibility.

EARPHONES: Using headphones or earphones while driving is prohibited, but speakers mounted inside a helmet are legal.

EXCESSIVE SPEED SANCTIONS: Florida has gotten tough with those who play speed and stunt games on the highways. Getting nicked for 50 mph or more over the limit will cost you $1,000 for the first offense, $2,500 for the second. Riding a motorcycle in which either wheel leaves the ground—that is, a wheelie or a stoppie—gets you the same treatment. You don't even want to know what happens if you get caught racing. Behave yourself.

EQUIPMENT REQUIREMENTS: A rearview mirror is required, as are a passenger seat and footrests if carrying a passenger.

ERRATICS: The law states that every motor vehicle must be equipped with two or more stop lamps. I've never seen more than one stop lamp on a stock motorcycle. Some law enforcement officers in Florida are convinced that a complete stop means that a rider puts both feet on the ground. There is nothing in Florida statute that confirms this—it says only "complete cessation of movement"—but beware.

GOOD RESOURCES

Florida Motor Vehicle Laws: http:www.leg.state.fl.us/statutes/
Florida Department of Highway Safety and Motor Vehicles: www.flhsmv.gov

GEORGIA

RIDEABILITY RANK: 44

With a higher ranking being best for motorcyclists, Georgia ranks 34th in the nation for population density and 41st for law enforcement density. Georgia is a warm mixture of two-lane mountain switchbacks and high-speed interstate expressways. Roadways tend to be curvy and crowned. The ratio of multi-vehicle motorcycle fatalities to single-vehicle motorcycle fatalities is 58/42. Georgia is known informally as a state notorious for writing traffic tickets. The typical patrol vehicle is a Ford Police Interceptor (Crown Vic) or Dodge Charger. The overall tone of law enforcement toward motorcycle riders is best described as businesslike.

GEORGIA LAWS IN DETAIL

Georgia uses a demerit points system to track driving records. Any adult driver who racks up 15 or more points within 24 months will get his or her license suspended. A speeding ticket 15–18 mph over will get you two points, 19–23 will get you three

GEORGIA AT A GLANCE

Helmet Law	Yes	Exhaust Noise	No
Eye Protection	Required by law	Earphones	Prohibited
Permit Restrictions	Yes	Checkpoints	Yes
Insurance	15/30/10	Automated Enforcement	Red light cameras
Reciprocity	No	School Buses	Yes
Handlebar Height Restriction	Yes	Pedestrians	Yes
Daytime Headlight Use	Required by law	Move-Over Law	Yes
Left Lane Restriction	No	Excessive Speed Sanctions	Yes
Unchanging Traffic Signal Law	No	Mandatory Tow	No
Turn Signals	Required by law	HOV	Okay
License Plate Display	No	Feet Down	No
Fenders	No	Erratics	Yes

For more detailed information on the above, see next page or reference Chapter 2: U.S. Motorcycle Laws and Regulations.

points, 24–33 will get you four points, and 34 mph or more will get you six. While it doesn't seem hard to avoid being suspended due to speeding, note that if you get suspended three times in five years, you're a habitual violator and they'll revoke your license for five years.

Drivers younger than 21 will be suspended for reckless, aggressive driving, a 24-mph-over-the-limit conviction, or any four-point violation. Drivers younger than 18 will be suspended if they accumulate four points within a 12-month period.

Interestingly, when your license is suspended due to an accumulation of points, the point total drops back down to zero once you have your license reinstated. And, once every five years, you can complete an approved driver improvement clinic for a reduction of up to seven points from your record.

HELMET LAW: Helmets meeting FMVSS 218 standards are required for all riders.

EYE PROTECTION: Unless you have a windshield, you must wear eye protection.

PERMIT RESTRICTIONS: Riders on a permit may operate during daylight hours only and may not carry passengers or travel upon limited-access highways.

RECIPROCITY: Georgia is not a member of the mostly nationwide Driver License Compact. The purpose of the compact is to assist states in administering the "one license, one driving record" concept. The only states remaining that don't adhere to the concept are Georgia, Massachusetts, Michigan, Tennessee, and Wisconsin. This doesn't mean that your home state won't find out about the ticket you received in one of these states, but it does mean you have a better chance of slipping by.

HANDLEBAR HEIGHT RESTRICTION: Handlebars can rise to a maximum of 15 inches above the operator's seat.

TURN SIGNALS: Electric turn signals are required on bikes built after 1972.

LICENSE PLATE DISPLAY: License plates are required to be fastened securely to prevent swinging and must be clearly visible.

EARPHONES: Use of headphones or earphones is prohibited, although communication devices are okay.

EXCESSIVE SPEED SANCTIONS: Georgia has a "super speeder" law that lumps an additional $200 onto any speeding ticket in which you are traveling 75 mph or more on a two-lane road or 85 mph or more on multi-lane roads.

EQUIPMENT REQUIREMENTS: At least one rearview mirror is required, and a passenger seat and footrests are required if carrying a passenger.

ERRATICS: Motorcycles are restricted from certain public and private areas. Callaway Gardens in Pine Mountain is one example. Atlantic Station in Atlanta is another.

GOOD RESOURCES

Department of Driver Services: www.dds.ga.gov/drivers/index.aspx
Rules and Regulations: www.sos.ga.gov/rules_regs.htm

HAWAII

RIDEABILITY RANK: 31

With a higher ranking being best for motorcyclists, Hawaii ranks 39th in the nation for population density and 27th for law enforcement density. Hawaii is a series of volcanic islands, some active, with extraordinary scenery. Roadways tend to be circuitous and in marginal condition. The ratio of multi-vehicle motorcycle fatalities to single-vehicle motorcycle fatalities is 51/49. The typical patrol vehicle is a Ford Police Interceptor (Crown Vic), but any vehicle can be used as a police car. Look for BMW motorcycles and, yes, even Toyotas. The overall tone of law enforcement toward motorcycle riders is best described as businesslike.

HAWAII AT A GLANCE

Helmet Law	Partial	Exhaust Noise	Yes
Eye Protection	Required by law	Earphones	Okay
Permit Restrictions	Yes	Checkpoints	Yes
Insurance	20/40/10,	Automated Enforcement	No
	No-fault	School Buses	Yes
Reciprocity	Yes	Pedestrians	Yes
Handlebar Height Restriction	Yes	Move-Over Law	Yes
Daytime Headlight Use	Not required	Excessive Speed Sanctions	Yes
Left Lane Restriction	No	Mandatory Tow	No
Unchanging Traffic Signal Law	No	HOV	Okay
Turn Signals	Required by law	Feet Down	No
License Plate Display	No	Erratics	None
Fenders	Yes, front and rear		

For more detailed information on the above, see next page or reference Chapter 2: U.S. Motorcycle Laws and Regulations.

HAWAII LAWS IN DETAIL

For minor violations, such as speeding tickets, there is no formal points system or "frequent flier" qualification system for license suspensions. However, more major infractions—such as no insurance, reckless, racing, etc.—can get you suspended. Whether or not to suspend your license based on the number or frequency of your moving violations is up to the court's discretion.

HELMET LAW: Partial. All riders and passengers under 18 are required to wear helmets that meet FMVSS 218 requirements.

EYE PROTECTION: Riders are required to have glasses, goggles, or a face shield, but it is up to law enforcement to determine what is acceptable. A suitable windscreen qualifies as eye protection if it is at least as high as the rider's eyes while seated and wide enough to deflect objects away from the rider's face.

PERMIT RESTRICTIONS: Riders on a permit cannot carry passengers or ride after dark.

HANDLEBAR HEIGHT RESTRICTION: Handlebars are permitted to rise no more than 15 inches above the operator's seat.

UNCHANGING TRAFFIC SIGNAL LAW: There is no law or affirmative defense that allows riders to proceed through an unchanging traffic signal, but it is common practice in Hawaii for motorcyclists to do so rather than wait for a light indefinitely. Law enforcement is aware of the problem and uses discretion when deciding whether or not to issue a citation.

EXHAUST NOISE: Riders cannot run mufflers that use a cutout or bypass or any mufflers that make more noise than the OEM unit.

EXCESSIVE SPEED SANCTIONS: If you're nicked for doing 30 mph over or more, or 80 mph anywhere, expect a fine of between $500 and $1,000 and a 30-day suspension. Also expect some time in school at a driver improvement clinic, jail time, or community service. Doing this twice within five years ups the ante significantly with minimum fines and a revoked license.

EQUIPMENT REQUIREMENTS: Motorcycles are required to have fenders front and rear, to have passenger seats and footrests if carrying passengers, and to receive annual inspections.

GOOD RESOURCES

Hawaii Department of Transportation: http://hawaii.gov/dot
Hawaii State Laws: www.capitol.hawaii.gov

IDAHO

RIDEABILITY RANK: 8

With a higher ranking being best for motorcyclists, Idaho ranks seventh in the nation for population density and 16th for law enforcement density. Idaho is a scenic river-valley, high-desert, and mountain state. Roadways tend to be curvy, rough at times, but always enjoyable. The ratio of multi-vehicle motorcycle fatalities to single-vehicle motorcycle fatalities is 47/53. The typical patrol vehicle is a Ford or Chevy SUV, Dodge Intrepid or Charger, or the ubiquitous Ford Police Interceptor (Crown Vic). The overall tone of law enforcement toward motorcycle riders is best described as businesslike.

IDAHO AT A GLANCE

Helmet Law	Partial		Exhaust Noise	Yes
Eye Protection	Not required		Earphones	Okay
Permit Restrictions	Yes		Checkpoints	No
Insurance	20/50/15		Automated Enforcement	No
Reciprocity	Yes		School Buses	Yes
Handlebar Height Restriction	None		Pedestrians	Yes
Daytime Headlight Use	Not required		Move-Over Law	Yes
Left Lane Restriction	None		Excessive Speed Sanctions	No
Unchanging Traffic Signal Law	Yes		Mandatory Tow	No
Turn Signals	Not required		Feet Down	No
License Plate Display	Yes		Erratics	None
Fenders	Required by law			

For more detailed information on the above, see next page or reference Chapter 2: U.S. Motorcycle Laws and Regulations.

IDAHO LAWS IN DETAIL

Idaho uses a demerit points system to track moving violations. Convictions are anywhere from one to four points. If you rack up 12 to 17 points in a 12-month period, expect to have your license suspended for 30 days. If you get 18 to 23 points within two years, it's a 90-day suspension. Getting nicked for 24 or more points in 36 months will get your license suspended for 180 days.

Idaho residents can enroll in a driver improvement clinic once every three years to have three points removed from their driving records.

HELMET LAW: All riders under 18 must wear helmets.

PERMIT RESTRICTIONS: Riders on permits cannot carry passengers or operate motorcycles on a freeway. Permitted riders can operate during daylight hours only.

UNCHANGING TRAFFIC SIGNAL LAW: If a traffic signal (red light) is deemed inoperative because it does not detect the presence of the motorcycle, it is permissible to proceed with caution as traffic allows. The rider must come to a complete stop and wait through at least one entire cycle of the traffic light before proceeding. However, language in the law states that this allowance does not apply to lights that do not have "detection" devices—e.g., those running on a timer. Be sure before you move.

TURN SIGNALS: While electric turn signals are not required on motorcycles, drivers are still obligated to signal turns, lane changes, etc., for at least five seconds on controlled-access highways and at least 100 feet everywhere else.

LICENSE PLATE DISPLAY: The plate must be securely fastened to prevent swinging and be mounted at a height of no less than 12 inches. It needs to be free from foreign materials and clearly legible (all letters and numbers visible).

FENDERS: Both front and rear fenders are required, and they must be at least as wide as the tires. The lowest part of the fender cannot be more than 20 inches from the ground.

EXHAUST NOISE: The law states that a muffler cannot increase engine noise to a level above that of the OEM muffler.

EQUIPMENT REQUIREMENTS: At least one rearview mirror is required, as are fenders front and rear. A passenger seat and footrests are required if you're carrying a passenger.

GOOD RESOURCES

Idaho Motor Vehicle Statutes: www.legislature.idaho.gov/idstat/Title49/T49.htm
Idaho Division of Motor Vehicles: www.itd.idaho.gov/dmv/

ILLINOIS

RIDEABILITY RANK: 45

With a higher ranking being best for motorcyclists, Illinois ranks 40th in the nation for population density and 46th for law enforcement density. Illinois is a plains state with heavy industry and a big city in the far north and rural, small-town prairie elsewhere in the south. Roadways tend to be flat, bumpy, and straight in the north, with rolling hills and curves in the south. The ratio of multi-vehicle motorcycle fatalities to single-vehicle motorcycle fatalities is 55/45. The typical patrol vehicle is a Ford Police Interceptor (Crown Vic) or Chevy Impala. The overall tone of law enforcement toward motorcycle riders is best described as businesslike.

ILLINOIS AT A GLANCE

Helmet Law	None	Earphones	Prohibited by law
Eye Protection	Required by law	Checkpoints	Yes
Permit Restrictions	Yes	Automated Enforcement	Speed, red light cameras, rail crossings
Insurance	20/40/15		
Reciprocity	Yes	School Buses	Yes
Handlebar Height Restriction	Yes	Pedestrians	Yes
Daytime Headlight Use	Required by law	Move-Over Law	Yes
Left Lane Restriction	Yes	Excessive Speed Sanctions	Yes
Unchanging Traffic Signal Law	No	Mandatory Tow	No
Turn Signals	Not required	HOV	Okay
License Plate Display	Yes	Feet Down	No
Fenders	Not required	Erratics	None
Exhaust Noise	No		

For more detailed information on the above, see next page or reference Chapter 2: U.S. Motorcycle Laws and Regulations.

ILLINOIS LAWS IN DETAIL

Illinois does not use a demerit points system to track moving violations. Any three moving violations within a 12-month period will get you suspended. If you're under 21, two violations in 24 months will get you suspended. Three convictions for reckless in a year can get you revoked, as can racing. Riding on one wheel is considered reckless driving.

HELMET LAW: Illinois is one of those few states with no helmet law whatsoever.

EYE PROTECTION: Both operators and passengers must wear glasses, goggles, or a face shield unless the motorcycle is equipped with a windscreen.

PERMIT RESTRICTIONS: Riders on permits must be under the direct supervision of a licensed operator 21 or older who has at least one year of riding experience. Permitted riders can ride only during daylight hours. Riders on permits who are younger than 18 can operate only "motor driven cycles," which are classified as less than 150 cc.

HANDLEBAR HEIGHT RESTRICTION: The handgrips must be below shoulder height while the rider is seated on the motorcycle.

LEFT LANE RESTRICTION: Slower traffic must use the right-hand lane. The left lane is for passing and turning only.

LICENSE PLATE DISPLAY: Any license plate cover is prohibited. License plate frames cannot cover any of the information on the plate.

EARPHONES: Headphones and/or earphones are prohibited. However, speakers mounted inside the helmet are okay if they are for communication purposes and not entertainment.

EXCESSIVE SPEED SANCTIONS: Speeding 40 mph or above the limit is a serious offense that carries the possibility of a year in jail, a $2,500 fine, or both. Speeding 30–39 over can get you six months in jail and a fine of $1,500 or both.

EQUIPMENT REQUIREMENTS: Motorcycles must bear at least one rearview mirror—and a passenger seat and footrests if carrying a passenger.

GOOD RESOURCES

Illinois Secretary of State: www.cyberdriveillinios.com
Illinois Statutes and Rules: www.ilga.gov

INDIANA

RIDEABILITY RANK: 24

With a higher ranking being best for motorcyclists, Indiana ranks 35th in the nation for population density and 9th for law enforcement density. Indiana is a Great Lakes state rich in history, scenic plains, and rolling hills. Roadways tend to be busy and flat. The ratio of multi-vehicle motorcycle fatalities to single-vehicle motorcycle fatalities is 58/42.The typical patrol vehicle is a Ford Police Interceptor (Crown Vic). Law enforcement also uses a surprising variety of forfeited vehicles—you can get stopped by a Dodge Neon, Chevy Pickup, or custom Pontiac Trans Am. The overall tone of law enforcement toward motorcycle riders is best described as businesslike.

INDIANA LAWS IN DETAIL

Indiana uses a points system for moving violations. You are assessed points after each conviction. Speeding 1–15 over will get you two points, 16–25 over will get you four, 26 or more will get you six points. A helmet or passenger violation will cost

INDIANA AT A GLANCE

Helmet Law	Partial	Exhaust Noise	Yes
Eye Protection	Required by law if under 18	Earphones	Okay
		Checkpoints	Yes
Permit Restrictions	Yes	Automated Enforcement	No
Insurance	25/50/10	School Buses	Yes
Reciprocity	Yes	Pedestrians	Yes
Handlebar Height Restriction	Yes	Move-Over Law	Yes
Daytime Headlight Use	Required by law	Excessive Speed Sanctions	Yes
Left Lane Restriction	No	Mandatory Tow	No
Unchanging Traffic Signal Law	Yes	Feet Down	No
Turn Signals	Required by law	Erratics	None
License Plate Display	Yes		
Fenders	No		

For more detailed information on the above, see next page or reference Chapter 2: U.S. Motorcycle Laws and Regulations.

you four points; disregarding a stop sign or stop light, failing to yield, or tailgating can cost you six; and failing to yield to an emergency vehicle or racing will get you eight. Accumulating 18 or more points in two years will get you an administrative hearing in which you can have your license suspended for up to a year, be put on probation for up to a year, or both. If you skip the hearing, they'll decide your fate without you. Indiana drivers can take a driver safety course that's good for four points off your record for three years. However, if you rack up two or more moving violation convictions in a year, you'll be required to take a driver safety course, without the benefit of reduced points.

Habitual violators who have one or more major violations (involving death, injury, DWI—even reckless driving) are subject to severe penalties if they rack up multiple convictions in a 10-year period. Depending on your record, you could have your license suspended for five or 10 years. For example, if you have two reckless tickets on your record and you get nicked for racing, you can kiss your license goodbye for 10 years. The same is true if you have nine speeding tickets and one school bus violation. Indiana doesn't mess around.

HELMET LAW: You must wear a DOT-compliant helmet if you are younger than 18 or if riding on an instruction permit.

EYE PROTECTION: Operators under 18 years of age are required to wear glasses, goggles, or a face shield.

PERMIT RESTRICTIONS: When riding on a permit, you may not carry a passenger, must wear a helmet, and cannot ride at night. If you are riding with an Indiana temporary motorcycle permit, you can ride only on the highway under the direct supervision of a licensed instructor.

HANDLEBAR HEIGHT RESTRICTION: This law recently changed from no more than 15 inches above the seat to no higher than the rider's shoulders.

TURN SIGNALS: Turn signals are required if your bike was manufactured in 1956 or later.

LICENSE PLATE: Your plate must be securely mounted, horizontal, and lighted, with no tinted cover.

EXHAUST NOISE: There is no special state law, but it should be noted that many cities have noise levels that they enforce on all vehicles.

AUTOMATED ENFORCEMENT: Indiana uses red light cameras and toll road checkpoints. If you proceed from one toll booth to the next in too short of a time, you can get a speeding ticket.

EQUIPMENT REQUIREMENTS: A working speedometer and at least one mirror is required. A passenger seat and footrests are required to carry a passenger.

GOOD RESOURCE
Indiana Bureau of Motor Vehicles: www.in.gov/bmv

IOWA

RIDEABILITY RANK: 4

With a higher ranking being best for motorcyclists, Iowa ranks 17th in the nation for population density and 5th for law enforcement density. Iowa is a scenic, motorcycle-friendly plains state with rolling farmland and wide-open spaces. Roadways tend to be flat, straight, and well maintained. The ratio of multi-vehicle motorcycle fatalities to single-vehicle motorcycle fatalities is 45/55. The typical patrol vehicle is a Ford Police Interceptor (Crown Vic) or Charger. The overall tone of law enforcement toward motorcycle riders is best described as indifferent.

IOWA LAWS IN DETAIL

Iowa does not use a demerit points system, except for serious habitual offenders dealing out life and death on the road. Being awarded three or more moving violations or being involved in three crashes in a 12-month period will get you sent to traffic school or suspended for five to 30 days. Any combination of these equaling three will also qualify you. "Excessive speeding" of 25 mph over or more, or in a police officer's

IOWA AT A GLANCE

Helmet Law	None		Exhaust Noise	No
Eye Protection	Not required		Earphones	Okay
Permit Restrictions	Yes		Checkpoints	No
Insurance	20/40/15		Automated Enforcement	Speed, red light cameras
Reciprocity	Yes		School Buses	Yes
Handlebar Height Restriction	Yes		Pedestrians	Yes
Daytime Headlight Use	Required by law		Move-Over Law	Yes
Left Lane Restriction	No		Excessive Speed Sanctions	Yes
Unchanging Traffic Signal Law	No		Mandatory Tow	No
Turn Signals	Not required		Feet Down	No
License Plate Display	Yes		Erratics	Yes
Fenders	Not required			

For more detailed information on the above, see next page or reference Chapter 2: U.S. Motorcycle Laws and Regulations.

view an unusually serious violation, will also get you thrown into school or suspended. After your driver improvement clinic, you'll be on probation for a year—and one more conviction will get you suspended during that time. Some speeding citations do not count toward your limits; see "Erratics" below.

"Careless" is generally seen as intentional and unnecessary showboating— wheelies, stoppies, skids, even swerving can be found here. Fleeing, racing, or two reckless convictions will get your license revoked. Six or more moving violations within two years (speeding violations have to be 15 mph over or more) will get you barred from driving for a year.

Iowa has a special ticket you can get for 10 mph over or less in 35- to 55-mph zones: It takes three of these to equal one citation for purposes of license suspension.

HELMET LAW: Iowa is one of three states with no helmet law whatsoever.
PERMIT RESTRICTIONS: The permit restrictions in Iowa are pretty minimal, requiring only supervision. A rider under 18 on an instruction permit must be in the presence of a licensed rider 21 or older who is an immediate family member or a guardian (or an adult 25 or older with parental permission). A rider who is 18 or older on a permit must be accompanied by an immediate family member who is a licensed rider or a licensed rider 25 or older.
HANDLEBAR HEIGHT RESTRICTION: Handlebars can rise to no more than 15 inches above the operator's seat.
DAYTIME HEADLIGHT USE: Headlights are required for bikes 1977 or newer.
TURN SIGNALS: Electric turn signals are not required, but drivers are required to signal turns 100 feet in advance at speeds less than 45 mph. At speeds over 45, the signal must be given at least 300 feet in advance.
LICENSE PLATE DISPLAY: Plates must face rearward and be mounted securely, and all numbers and letters must be in full view (no license plate frames).
EQUIPMENT REQUIREMENTS: At least one rearview mirror is required, as is a fender at the rear. A passenger seat and footrests are required if carrying a passenger, and motorcycles must have a working speedometer and odometer.
ERRATICS: Certain speeding violations are not counted for driver improvement clinic or suspension reasons. In a 12-month period, the first two convictions of 10 mph or less over the limit in 35- to 55-mph zones don't count against you.

GOOD RESOURCES
Iowa Department of Transportation: www.iowadot.gov
Code of Iowa Section 321: www.legis.state.ia.us/IACODE/2001SUPPLEMENT/321/index.htm

KANSAS

RIDEABILITY RANK: 20

With a higher ranking being best for motorcyclists, Kansas ranks
11th in the nation for population density and 39th for law
enforcement density. Kansas is a long, rural plains state with plenty
of deer. The populace is very accepting of motorcyclists. Roadways
tend to be never-ending, flat, and straight—with some memorable,
curvy exceptions. Roads are generally well maintained. The ratio of
multi-vehicle motorcycle fatalities to single-vehicle motorcycle
fatalities is 50/50. The typical patrol vehicle is a Ford Police
Interceptor (Crown Vic), Dodge Charger, or sometimes a Chevy SUV.
The overall tone of law enforcement toward motorcycle riders is best
described as businesslike.

KANSAS AT A GLANCE

Helmet Law	Partial	Exhaust Noise	No
Eye Protection	Required by law	Earphones	Okay
Permit Restrictions	Yes	Checkpoints	Yes
Insurance	25/50/10, No-fault	Automated Enforcement	No
		School Buses	Yes
Reciprocity	No	Pedestrians	Yes
Handlebar Height Restriction	None	Move-Over Law	Yes
Daytime Headlight Use	Required by law	Excessive Speed Sanctions	Yes
Left Lane Restriction	Yes	Mandatory Tow	No
Unchanging Traffic Signal Law	No	HOV	No
Turn Signals	Required by law	Feet Down	No
License Plate Display	No	Erratics	None
Fenders	Not required		

For more detailed information on the above, see next page or reference Chapter 2: U.S. Motorcycle Laws and Regulations.

KANSAS LAWS IN DETAIL

Kansas doesn't use a points system for license sanctions. Reckless driving and fleeing will get your license revoked. If you rack up three or more moving violation convictions within a 12-month period, you'll get a letter telling you your license has been suspended. The state also reserves the right, if you acquire moving violations with unusual frequency, to suspend your license outside of the three-in-12-months threshold. Kansas law does allow for reinstating a suspended license if an individual participates in a defensive driving course, though this is approved on a case-by-case basis.

HELMET LAW: Operators and passengers under 18 must wear DOT-compliant helmets.

EYE PROTECTION: Passengers under 18 and all operators are required to wear glasses, goggles, or a face shield—or else have a windshield with a minimum height of 10 inches (measured from the center of the handlebars).

PERMIT RESTRICTIONS: A rider operating on an instruction permit must be accompanied by an adult on a motorcycle with a motorcycle endorsement.

LEFT LANE RESTRICTION: Except inside of city limits, the left lane is for passing. You can be ticketed.

TURN SIGNALS: You must signal turns and lane changes within 100 feet. Every motorcycle manufactured after January 1, 1973, shall be equipped with electric turn signals.

AUTOMATED ENFORCEMENT: Kansas uses red light cameras and speed cameras in some jurisdictions.

EXCESSIVE SPEED SANCTIONS: I believe that 25 over the limit will get you a trip to jail.

EQUIPMENT REQUIREMENTS: Motorcycles are required to have one red reflector at the rear, and at least one left-hand mirror is required. A passenger seat and footrests are required to carry a passenger, and motorcycles may be required to submit to a random inspection.

ERRATICS: Passing or overtaking within 100 feet of an emergency or highway construction vehicle with lights flashing is prohibited. Speeding at less than 80 mph in a 70-mph zone is not an offense that goes on your record.

GOOD RESOURCES

Kansas Department of Revenue: www.ksrevenue.org/pdf/dlhb.pdf
Kansas Legislature: www.kslegislature.org/legsrv-statutes/index.do

KENTUCKY

RIDEABILITY RANK: 11

With a higher ranking being best for motorcyclists, Kentucky ranks 30th in the nation for population density and sixth for law enforcement density. Kentucky is a bluegrass pasture state with plateaus, winding roads, and rolling hills. Roadways tend to be narrow and sinuous. The ratio of multi-vehicle motorcycle fatalities to single-vehicle motorcycle fatalities is 47/53. The typical patrol vehicle is a Ford Police Interceptor (Crown Vic). The overall tone of law enforcement toward motorcycle riders is best described as businesslike.

KENTUCKY AT A GLANCE

Helmet Law	Partial	Fenders	Not required
Eye Protection	Required by law	Exhaust Noise	No
Permit Restrictions	Yes	Earphones	Okay
Insurance	25/50/10, No-fault optional	Checkpoints	Yes
		Automated Enforcement	No
Reciprocity	Yes	School Buses	Yes
Handlebar Height Restriction	None	Pedestrians	Yes
Daytime Headlight Use	Not required	Move-Over Law	Yes
Left Lane Restriction	Yes	Excessive Speed Sanctions	No
Unchanging Traffic Signal Law	No	Mandatory Tow	No
Turn Signals	Required by law	Feet Down	No
License Plate Display	No	Erratics	Yes

For more detailed information on the above, see next page or reference Chapter 2: U.S. Motorcycle Laws and Regulations.

KENTUCKY LAWS IN DETAIL

Kentucky uses a demerit points system to track moving violations. Any driver accumulating six points gets the attention of the Division of Driver Licensing (DDL) and may be required to attend a driver improvement clinic. Collecting 12 points in two years could mean you're suspended for six months (six points for drivers under 18). A second suspension will get you at least a year's suspension; the third and additional suspensions run for two years. It is possible to be placed on probation instead of taking a suspension, which usually involves participation in a driver improvement clinic. This is also a way of keeping violation points off your driving record—if the state deems you eligible for this.

Speeding up to 10 mph over on a limited-access highway carries no points. Traveling 11–15 over on a limited-access highway will get you three points, as will speeding convictions on other roads up to 15 mph over the limit. Getting nicked for 16–24 mph will get you six points, while reckless is worth four. Points assessed from a conviction remain on your record for two years, though the conviction remains on your record for five years. Racing, fleeing, or speeding 26 mph or more over the limit will get you a 90-day suspension. Three reckless convictions in 12 months can get you suspended or revoked.

HELMET LAW: The law requires that all riders must wear helmets that meet FMVSS 218 standards, unless they are 21 or older and have had a motorcycle license for at least one year. Passengers are required to be 21 or older to ride without helmets.

EYE PROTECTION: Riders must wear glasses, goggles, or a face shield.

PERMIT RESTRICTIONS: A helmet is required, and a rider on a permit cannot carry passengers.

TURN SIGNALS: Electric turn signals are required by law if the motorcycle came originally equipped with them.

SCHOOL BUSES: A standard stop-for-school-bus law also applies to church buses in Kentucky.

EQUIPMENT REQUIREMENTS: Motorcycles are required to carry at least one rearview mirror, and a passenger seat and footrests are required if carrying a passenger.

GOOD RESOURCES

Kentucky Transportation Cabinet: http://transportation.ky.gov
Kentucky State Statutes: www.lrc.ky.gov

LOUISIANA

RIDEABILITY RANK: 41

With a higher ranking being best for motorcyclists, Louisiana ranks 28th in the nation for population density and (almost) dead last at 50th for law enforcement density (tied with the District of Columbia, but there really is no comparison). While rural upland, Louisiana is a river-delta state with swamps, coastal marshes, and bayous. Roadways tend to be flat, narrow, and gently curving. The ratio of multi-vehicle motorcycle fatalities to single-vehicle motorcycle fatalities is 54/46. The typical patrol vehicle is a Ford Police Interceptor (Crown Vic) or Chevy Impala. Chargers and SUVs are not uncommon. The overall tone of law enforcement toward motorcycle riders is best described as businesslike, but the state is known for aggressive speed traps.

LOUISIANA AT A GLANCE

Helmet Law	Yes		Exhaust Noise	No
Eye Protection	Required by law		Earphones	One ear only
Permit Restrictions	None (Graduated Driver Licensing)		Checkpoints	Yes
Insurance	10/20/10		Automated Enforcement	Speed, red light cameras
Reciprocity	Yes		School Buses	Yes
Handlebar Height Restriction	Yes		Pedestrians	Yes
Daytime Headlight Use	Not required		Move-Over Law	No
Left Lane Restriction	Yes		Excessive Speed Sanctions	No
Unchanging Traffic Signal Law	No		HOV	Okay
Turn Signals	Required by law		Mandatory Tow	No
License Plate Display	No		Feet Down	No
Fenders	Not required		Erratics	None

For more detailed information on the above, see next page or reference Chapter 2: U.S. Motorcycle Laws and Regulations.

LOUISIANA LAWS IN DETAIL

Louisiana does not use a demerit points system to track moving violations, and it appears that you have to be a pretty bad person to get your license suspended. There are no state-set fees; the cost of a moving violation is set by the local jurisdictions (cities and parishes). Some parishes have education programs in which your violation is dismissed if you complete a driver improvement clinic, which costs about the same as a modest speeding ticket. Convictions remain on your record for five years.

Three convictions of reckless driving committed within a 12-month period can easily get you a suspension. The same goes for failing to stop for a school bus or failing to answer a citation. Violating a restriction on your license is also good grounds for suspension.

You will get your license suspended for three years if you are convicted of three major violations in any state, such as DWI, hit-and-run, and driving after suspension within five years. Your license can also be suspended for three years for 10 major and/or minor violations (speeding, etc.) in any state within three years.

HELMET LAW: FMVSS 218–compliant helmets are mandatory for all riders.

EYE PROTECTION: It is not legal to use tinted eyewear at night. Glasses, goggles, or face shields must meet state requirements. Eye protection is not required if the motorcycle is equipped with a windshield that is tall enough to provide adequate protection and meets state requirements.

PERMIT RESTRICTIONS: Louisiana does not have a motorcycle instruction permit process. However, minors 15 or 16 years old on instruction permits have to remain within three miles of home and cannot ride between 11 p.m. and 5 a.m. unless accompanied by a licensed adult. If you're riding in Louisiana on a motorcycle permit, your best bet is to remain within the restrictions of your home state.

HANDLEBAR HEIGHT RESTRICTION: Handlebars can be no more than 15 inches above the operator's seat.

LEFT LANE RESTRICTION: On an uncongested multi-lane roadway, you must use the right lane. You may use the left lane only for passing or turning.

TURN SIGNALS: Electric turn signals are required for bikes manufactured in 1973 and later. Regardless of whether you have electric turn signals, you still have to signal when you plan to turn, change lanes, slow down, or stop—at least 100 feet in advance.

EARPHONES: Operators can use headphones/earphones in one ear only. Speakers mounted inside the helmet are okay.

AUTOMATED ENFORCEMENT: Some Louisiana municipalities use red light cameras and speed cameras. Vehicle-mounted cameras have been reported to be in use, as well.

EQUIPMENT REQUIREMENTS: A left-side rearview mirror is required, and a passenger seat and footrests are required to carry a passenger. Bikes are subject to annual inspections.

GOOD RESOURCES

Louisiana Office of Motor Vehicles: http://omv.dps.state.la.us
Louisiana State Laws Title 32: http://www.legis.state.la.us

MAINE

RIDEABILITY RANK: 5

With a higher ranking being best for motorcyclists, Maine ranks 13th in the nation for population density and 10th for law enforcement density. Maine is a scenic coastal state with river valleys, lakes, and mountain foothills. Roadways tend to defer to the area topography rather than blasting straight through it. Rumor has it, however, that Maine's roads are not as well maintained as those in other New England states. The ratio of multi-vehicle motorcycle fatalities to single-vehicle motorcycle fatalities is 45/55. The typical patrol vehicle is a Ford Police Interceptor (Crown Vic), though there are a few Chevy Impalas and various SUVs in the fleets. The overall tone of law enforcement toward motorcycle riders is best described as businesslike.

MAINE AT A GLANCE

Helmet Law	Partial		Exhaust Noise	Yes
Eye Protection	Not required		Earphones	Okay
Permit Restrictions	Yes		Checkpoints	Yes
Insurance	50/100/25		Automated Enforcement	No
Reciprocity	Yes		School Buses	Yes
Handlebar Height Restriction	Yes		Pedestrians	Yes
Daytime Headlight Use	Required by law		Move-Over Law	Yes
Left Lane Restriction	Yes		Excessive Speed Sanctions	No
Unchanging Traffic Signal Law	No		Mandatory Tow	No
Turn Signals	Not required		Feet Down	No
License Plate Display	Yes		Erratics	None
Fenders	Yes			

MAINE LAWS IN DETAIL

Maine uses a demerit points system. Six points gets you a warning, and 12 gets you a suspension. Points fall off the driving record after one year. A good driving record with no violations gets you one free "credit" point a year, up to a maximum of four points at a time, to offset or negate points accumulated with moving violations. Completing a driver improvement course will remove three points from your record and can be done once a year.

Major violations get you six points. Minor violations get you two to four points. A speeding conviction of 15–29 mph over the limit gets you six points, while 1–15 mph over will get you four points. If your license gets suspended three times in three years, you may get an additional suspension of 120 days. "Driving to endanger" (reckless/careless) will get you suspended for 30 days immediately (12 points). Racing can get you suspended for 90 days. Traveling 30 mph or more over the speed limit can get you suspended for 30 days.

HELMET LAW: Maine has a partial helmet law, requiring helmets for riders younger than 18 and those who have had a motorcycle license less than one year. Helmets are also required for riders with instruction permits. If a rider is required to wear a helmet, the passenger is required to wear one.

PERMIT RESTRICTIONS: Helmets are mandatory. Riders can ride during daylight hours only, and they cannot carry passengers.

HANDLEBAR HEIGHT RESTRICTION: Handlebars must be below shoulder height when the driver is seated on the bike.

LICENSE PLATE DISPLAY: Motorcycle plates must be mounted horizontally on the rearmost part of the rear fender.

FENDERS: Fenders, both front and rear, are required on motorcycles.

EXHAUST NOISE: Bikes are required to run an adequate muffler that is properly maintained to prevent excessive or unusual noise—including noise that is noticeably louder than other similar vehicles. Modification to an exhaust system to make it louder than stock is prohibited.

EQUIPMENT REQUIREMENTS: At least one rearview mirror is required, and a passenger seat and footrests are required to carry a passenger. Amber reflectors up front and red reflectors on the rear (sides) are required, as is one facing rearward. Be prepared to have them on the bike when the annual equipment and safety inspection comes around.

GOOD RESOURCE
Maine.gov: www.maine.gov

MARYLAND

RIDEABILITY RANK: 48

With a higher ranking being best for motorcyclists, Maryland ranks 46th in the nation for population density and 42nd for law enforcement density. Maryland, sometimes known as "America in Miniature," is a state with wide variety, from sandy dunes to low wetlands, mountains, and forests. Roadways tend to be well maintained with good signage. The ratio of multi-vehicle motorcycle fatalities to single-vehicle motorcycle fatalities is 60/40. The typical patrol vehicle is a Ford Police Interceptor (Crown Vic), SUV, or Charger. The overall tone of law enforcement toward motorcycle riders is best described as enthusiastic.

MARYLAND AT A GLANCE

Helmet Law	Yes		Exhaust Noise	No
Eye Protection	Required by law		Earphones	One ear only
Permit Restrictions	Yes		Checkpoints	Yes
Insurance	20/40/10		Automated Enforcement	Speed, red light cameras
Reciprocity	Yes			
Handlebar Height Restriction	Yes		School Buses	Yes
Daytime Headlight Use	Not required		Pedestrians	Yes
Left Lane Restriction	None		Move-Over Law	Yes
Unchanging Traffic Signal Law	None		Excessive Speed Sanctions	No
Turn Signals	Not required		Mandatory Tow	No
License Plate Display	Yes		HOV	Okay
Fenders	Required by law		Feet Down	No
			Erratics	Yes

For more detailed information on the above, see next page or reference Chapter 2: U.S. Motorcycle Laws and Regulations.

MARYLAND LAWS IN DETAIL

Maryland uses a demerit points system to track moving violations. Upon reaching five points, you'll get invited to a "conference" to discuss your driving behavior and must complete a driver improvement clinic. Once you reach eight points, your license will be suspended. At 12 points, your license will be revoked. When you're convicted of a moving violation, the points remain on your record for two years.

Speeding 10 mph or more above the limit will cost you two points. Speeding at 30 mph or more over the limit, or 20 or more over the limit in a 65-mph zone, will each get you five points. Any moving violation that contributes to an accident is three points. Racing is worth five, and reckless is worth six. It is worth noting that if you receive multiple citations at the same time, only the conviction with the highest points goes toward your point total, although all convictions will remain on your record.

HELMET LAW: Helmets that meet FMVSS 218 standards are required for all riders and passengers regardless of age or license status.

EYE PROTECTION: Glasses, goggles, or a face shield is required for riders and passengers if the bike does not have a windscreen high enough to protect the face.

PERMIT RESTRICTIONS: Riders on a permit must be under the direct supervision of a licensed motorcyclist 21 or older who has at least three years of riding experience. The only passenger you can carry is a licensed motorcyclist—presumably the one who is supervising you.

HANDLEBAR HEIGHT RESTRICTION: Handgrips may not exceed a height of 15 inches above the operator's seat.

TURN SIGNALS: Even though turn signals are not required, you are required by law to signal your turn or lane change.

LICENSE PLATE DISPLAY: The plate must be free of obstructions or foreign materials, clearly legible, securely fastened in a manner that prevents the plate from swinging, in a horizontal position, and placed so as to be clearly visible.

EQUIPMENT REQUIREMENTS: Two rearview mirrors are required left and right, and front and rear fenders are required. A passenger seat, footrests, and handholds are required to carry a passenger. A working speedometer and odometer are mandated, and an inspection is required when you transfer the vehicle title.

ERRATICS: While it is legal for two riders to ride side-by-side within a lane, it is not legal for one rider to pass another within a single lane. Also, Maryland law states that it's illegal to remove any safety device or equipment that is required by federal vehicle code and came stock with the motorcycle—such as a big, gaudy reflector.

GOOD RESOURCE

Maryland Motor Vehicle Administration: www.mva.maryland.gov

MASSACHUSETTS

RIDEABILITY RANK: 43

With a higher ranking being best for motorcyclists, Massachusetts ranks 48th in the nation for population density and 43rd for law enforcement density. Massachusetts is a historic state with urban coastal areas, rural uplands, and low mountains. Roadways tend to be narrow and follow the topography of the land around them. The ratio of multi-vehicle motorcycle fatalities to single-vehicle motorcycle fatalities is 51/49. Massachusetts is known informally as a state notorious for writing traffic tickets. The typical patrol vehicle is a Ford Police Interceptor (Crown Vic), though the state police have an impressive array of Harley-Davidsons. The overall tone of law enforcement toward motorcycle riders is best described as businesslike.

MASSACHUSETTS AT A GLANCE

Helmet Law	Yes		Exhaust Noise	No
Eye Protection	Required by law		Earphones	Prohibited by law
Permit Restrictions	Yes		Checkpoints	Yes
Insurance	20/40/5, No-fault		Automated Enforcement	Speed
Reciprocity	No		School Buses	Yes
Handlebar Height Restriction	Yes		Pedestrians	Yes
Daytime Headlight Use	Not required		Move-Over Law	Yes
Left Lane Restriction	Yes		Excessive Speed Sanctions	No
Unchanging Traffic Signal Law	No		Mandatory Tow	No
Turn Signals	Required by law		HOV	Okay
License Plate Display	Yes		Feet Down	No
Fenders	Required by law		Erratics	Yes

For more detailed information on the above, see next page or reference Chapter 2: U.S. Motorcycle Laws and Regulations.

MASSACHUSETTS LAWS IN DETAIL

Massachusetts does not use a points system to track moving violations. Moving violations and at-fault crashes count against you when determining whether or not to let you drive anymore based on your driving record.

The lowest amount you'll pay for speeding is $100. All speeding convictions also include a $50 surcharge. When you're more than 10 mph over the speed limit, you'll pay an extra $10 for each mile per hour above 10. Three speeding convictions and/or at-fault crashes in 12 months will get you suspended for 30 days. More than that gets you suspended for a year. At-fault crashes also include a $50 surcharge.

Three surchargeable events in a two-year period may also get you a license suspension. A third will get you a mandatory driver improvement clinic, and every subsequent surchargeable event will get you another trip to school, no matter how many times you've taken the course. Habitual traffic offenders—that is, three major moving violations or any combination of 12 moving violations in five years—should expect to have their licenses suspended for four years.

HELMET LAW: All riders and passengers are required to wear helmets that meet the requirements of FMVSS 218.

EYE PROTECTION: Motorcycle operators must wear eyeglasses, goggles, or a helmet face shield if the motorcycle does not have a windshield or windscreen.

PERMIT RESTRICTIONS: Riders operating under a motorcycle permit may not carry passengers or ride at night.

RECIPROCITY: Massachusetts is not a member of the mostly nationwide Driver License Compact. The purpose of the compact is to assist states in administering the "one license, one driving record" concept. The only states remaining that don't adhere to the concept are Georgia, Massachusetts, Michigan, Tennessee, and Wisconsin. This doesn't mean that your home state won't find out about the ticket you received in one of these states, but it does mean you have a better chance of slipping by if you do.

HANDLEBAR HEIGHT RESTRICTION: Handlebars can rise no greater than 15 inches above the operator's seat, and they must be below shoulder height.

LEFT LANE RESTRICTION: Use the right lane on a multi-lane highway unless you are making a pass or a left turn or unless the right lane is blocked.

TURN SIGNALS: Mechanical turn signals are required on motorcycles 1973 or newer.

LICENSE PLATE DISPLAY: Plates must be undamaged, securely mounted on the rear, clean, and clearly visible. No accessories (including plate frame) can obstruct the plate.

EQUIPMENT REQUIREMENTS: At least one rearview mirror is required. Fenders are required at both front and rear, and a passenger seat and footrests are required to carry a passenger. An annual inspection is also required.

ERRATICS: Boston has a motorcycle exhaust/noise ordinance that effectively requires an EPA stamp on every motorcycle exhaust. The penalty for noncompliance is a ticket for $300.

GOOD RESOURCES

Massachusetts Registry of Motor Vehicles: www.massdot.state.ma.us/rmv/
Massachusetts Motor Vehicle Laws Chapter 90: www.malegislature.gov

MICHIGAN

RIDEABILITY RANK: 26

With a higher ranking being best for motorcyclists, Michigan ranks 36th in the nation for population density and 11th for law enforcement density. Michigan is a scenic lakefront, farming, and forested state. Roadways tend to be flat, rough, and curvy. The ratio of multi-vehicle motorcycle fatalities to single-vehicle motorcycle fatalities is 57/43. The typical patrol vehicles are Ford Police Interceptors (Crown Vics) and Chevy Impalas, with a few SUVs and Chargers here and there. The overall tone of law enforcement toward motorcycle riders is best described as businesslike.

MICHIGAN LAWS IN DETAIL

Michigan uses a demerit points system. Ten points will get your license suspended. A reckless, fleeing, or first-time DUI is worth six points. Drag racing, driving impaired, and 16 or more mph over the limit will get you four. Careless or speeding 11–15 over

MICHIGAN AT A GLANCE

Helmet Law	Yes	Exhaust Noise	Yes
Eye Protection	Partial	Earphones	Okay
Permit Restrictions	Yes	Checkpoints	No
Insurance	20/40/10, No-fault	Automated Enforcement	No
		School Buses	Yes
Reciprocity	No	Pedestrians	No
Handlebar Height Restriction	Yes	Move-Over Law	Yes
Daytime Headlight Use	Not required	Excessive Speed Sanctions	Yes
Left Lane Restriction	Yes	Mandatory Tow	No
Unchanging Traffic Signal Law	No	HOV	Okay
Turn Signals	Not required	Feet Down	No
License Plate Display	Yes	Erratics	Yes
Fenders	Not required		

For more detailed information on the above, see next page or reference Chapter 2: U.S. Motorcycle Laws and Regulations.

will get you three. Most other minor infractions and 10 mph over or less will get you two points. Points remain on your record until two years after the conviction. Reckless driving will get you a 90-day suspension.

There do not appear to be any administrative sanctions for "habitual offenders" like in many other states (such as X number of violations within Y time period equals mandatory suspension). As long as your infractions are minor and you remain below 10 points, you will retain your privilege to ride. Michiganders with relatively good records can have points waived by completing a driver improvement clinic. To qualify for this safety course, you must have no more than two points already on your record, and you still must pay the ticket and the fee for the course. But if your goal is to keep your record clean, it's worth the money.

Michigan is not a member of the Nonresident Violator Compact (NRVC), which is meant to ensure equal treatment of nonresidents and residents and standardize methods for processing citations, as well as the response of the rider/driver to comply to them. This means that if you're nabbed for a moving violation here, the arresting officer is not obligated to release you without posting bond for the fine. If you don't have a method of posting bond (cash works; checks and credit may work), you could end up in jail until you do. And, if you are required to pay the fine or appear in court and fail to do so, your home state will not necessarily suspend your license until you comply with the citation's requirements (pay the fine). In fact, they may never even know about it. States that are not members of this compact are Alaska, California, Michigan, Montana, Oregon, and Wisconsin.

EYE PROTECTION: Eye protection is required when traveling at speeds 35 mph or greater. If your bike has a windshield or windscreen, this will suffice.

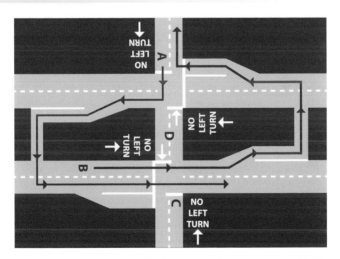

The "Michigan Left Turn" was developed in the 1960s to improve safety and traffic flow on divided highways (see Erratics on the next page).

PERMIT RESTRICTIONS: Riders on temporary instruction permits cannot ride at night or carry passengers. Permit riders must be under constant visual supervision of a licensed rider 18 or older.

RECIPROCITY: Michigan is not a member of the mostly nationwide Driver License Compact. The purpose of the compact is to assist states in administering the "one license, one driving record" concept. The only states remaining that don't adhere to the concept are Georgia, Massachusetts, Michigan, Tennessee, and Wisconsin. This doesn't mean that your home state won't find out about the ticket you received in one of these states, but it does mean you have a better chance of slipping by.

HANDLEBAR HEIGHT RESTRICTION: The maximum height for motorcycle handlebars is 15 inches above the lowest point of the "un-depressed" seat.

LEFT LANE RESTRICTION: Drivers are required to stay in the right lane except when passing another vehicle or an emergency vehicle on the shoulder.

TURN SIGNALS: Even though electric turn signals are not required on motorcycles, riders are still required to signal turns (hand signals).

LICENSE PLATE DISPLAY: Plates must be attached securely to prevent swinging, and they must be horizontal. They must also be at least 12 inches from the ground and clear of debris (plainly visible).

EXHAUST NOISE: Many local ordinances that regulate exhaust noise are enforced across Michigan.

EXCESSIVE SPEED SANCTIONS: Reckless driving is taken seriously, with up to 93 days in jail and a $500 fine for a conviction. While defined as "willful or wanton disregard," this is something open to interpretation by law enforcement. Be thoughtful.

EQUIPMENT REQUIREMENTS: A rearview mirror and front and rear brakes are required. A passenger seat and footrests are required if you're carrying a passenger. Michigan does conduct random vehicle inspections.

ERRATICS: The "Michigan Left Turn" (or boulevard turnaround) was developed in the 1960s to improve safety and traffic flow for motorists turning left onto, or left off of, a divided highway. In more than 700 locations statewide, traffic using a divided highway cannot turn left at a crossroad. Instead, drivers pass the crossroad and use a left turn lane and median crossover several hundred feet past the intersection—essentially, you pass the intersection, complete a U-turn at a crossover, and then head back the other direction and make a right turn instead. Drivers at a crossroads who want to turn left onto a divided highway have to instead make a right turn, then a U-turn in the crossover.

GOOD RESOURCES

Michigan Vehicle Code: www.michigan.gov/msp
Michigan Motorcycle Manual: www.michigan.gov/sos

MINNESOTA

RIDEABILITY RANK: 7

With a higher ranking being best for motorcyclists, Minnesota ranks 21st in the nation for population density and third for law enforcement density. Minnesota is a scenic river-valley, lakes, and prairie state. Roadways tend to be wide, flat, and straight, except in river valleys, where they are wide, flat, and curvy. The ratio of multi-vehicle motorcycle fatalities to single-vehicle motorcycle fatalities is 47/53. The typical patrol vehicle is a Ford Crown Vic or Chevy Impala. The overall tone of law enforcement toward motorcycle riders is best described as businesslike.

MINNESOTA LAWS IN DETAIL

Minnesota does not use a points system for driving records. If you are convicted of three traffic violations within a one-year period, or four violations within a two-year period, you receive a warning letter from the DMV. Four violations within a one-year

MINNESOTA AT A GLANCE

Helmet Law	Partial	Exhaust Noise	Yes
Eye Protection	Required by law	Earphones	One ear only
Permit Restrictions	Yes	Checkpoints	No
Insurance	30/60/10, No-fault	Automated Enforcement	No
		School Buses	Yes
Reciprocity	Yes	Pedestrians	Yes
Handlebar Height Restriction	None	Move-Over Law	Yes
Daytime Headlight Use	Required by law	Excessive Speed Sanctions	Yes
Left Lane Restriction	No	Mandatory Tow	No
Unchanging Traffic Signal Law	Yes		
Turn Signals	Not required	HOV	Okay
License Plate Display	Yes	Feet Down	No
Fenders	Not required	Erratics	Yes

For more detailed information on the above, see next page or reference Chapter 2: U.S. Motorcycle Laws and Regulations.

period or five violations within a two-year period gets your license suspended for 30 days. If you are convicted of five violations within a one-year period or six violations within a two-year period, your license will be suspended for 90 days. Seven violations in a two-year period will get you a 180-day suspension; eight will get you a year.

HELMET LAW: DOT-compliant helmets are required for riders younger than 18 and those holding motorcycle instruction permits.

EYE PROTECTION: Eye protection—glasses, goggles, or a face shield—is required for the operator but not the passenger.

PERMIT RESTRICTIONS: A helmet is required. The operator is not allowed to carry passengers, ride on interstate freeways, or ride at night.

UNCHANGING TRAFFIC SIGNAL LAW: Motorcyclists have an "affirmative defense" for red light violations. This means a rider can still receive a citation for blowing off a red light but has a standard, accepted defense. This involves proving that you 1) came to a complete stop, 2) waited an unreasonable time, 3) decided the light was either malfunctioning or did not recognize you, and 4) proceeded only when safe to do so.

LICENSE PLATE DISPLAY: The motorcycle plate must be securely fastened, clearly visible, and mounted horizontally. No funky angle mounts are allowed, nor are any plate frames or clear covers that obstruct, even partially, any letter or number on the plate or tag. Plates must be mounted horizontally, unless you have a special, state-issued vertical plate specifically for a motorcycle.

EXHAUST NOISE: Minnesota uses standard language but also includes "no sharp popping or crackling sound."

EARPHONES: Wearing an earphone is restricted to one ear only, although helmet-mounted speakers are okay.

EXCESSIVE SPEED SANCTIONS: Expect additional fines for speeding tickets 20 mph or more above the posted limit. And like most states, fines double in construction zones. Speeding in excess of 100 mph will get your driving privileges suspended for six months.

REQUIRED EQUIPMENT: At least one mirror is required, and a passenger seat and footrests are required if carrying a passenger.

ERRATICS: An unusual law prevents certain speeding violations from ever reaching Minnesotans' driving records. A driver who is cited for going no greater than 10 mph over in a 55-mph zone, or no more than 5 over in a 60 zone, qualifies. This law doesn't apply to commercial vehicles. Another law requires passengers to be large enough to reach both footrests while seated on the passenger seat.

GOOD RESOURCES
Minnesota Department of Public Safety: www.dps.state.mn.us
Minnesota Statutes: www.revisor.mn.gov

MISSISSIPPI

RIDEABILITY RANK: 34

With a higher ranking being best for motorcyclists, Mississippi ranks 16th in the nation for population density and 31st for law enforcement density. Mississippi is a river delta state with heavy forests, coastal plains, and rolling foothills. The ratio of multi-vehicle motorcycle fatalities to single-vehicle motorcycle fatalities is 52/48. The typical patrol vehicle is a Ford Police Interceptor (Crown Vic). The overall tone of law enforcement toward motorcycle riders is best described as businesslike.

MISSISSIPPI AT A GLANCE

Helmet Law	Yes	Exhaust Noise	No
Eye Protection	Not required	Earphones	Okay
Permit Restrictions	None	Checkpoints	Yes
Insurance	25/50/25	Automated Enforcement	No
Reciprocity	Yes	School Buses	Yes
Handlebar Height Restriction	None	Pedestrians	Yes
Daytime Headlight Use	Not required	Move-Over Law	Yes
Left Lane Restriction	None	Excessive Speed Sanctions	No
Unchanging Traffic Signal Law	None	Mandatory Tow	No
Turn Signals	Not required	Feet Down	No
License Plate Display	No	Erratics	Yes
Fenders	Rear required		

For more detailed information on the above, see next page or reference Chapter 2: U.S. Motorcycle Laws and Regulations.

MISSISSIPPI LAWS IN DETAIL

Mississippi does not use a demerit points system to track moving violations, nor is there any set thresholds for how many speeding or moving violations get your license suspended. The decision whether or not to suspend your license will be up to the courts or the Department of Public Safety. Penalties for convictions are up to 10 days in jail and $100 for a first offense in a year; up to 20 days in jail and $200 for the second offense in a year; and up to six months in jail and $500 for a third offense in a year.

Driving conviction records are held for three years. Habitual recklessness or frequent convictions for moving violations will get you suspended. Three reckless convictions in a year will get you revoked. Driver improvement clinics are alive and well in Mississippi, and they may be used to avoid having a citation placed on your record if it's the first in three years.

HELMET LAW: Helmets are required for all operators and passengers. Compliance is described as meeting the requirements of the American Association of Motor Vehicle Administrators, which cites FMVSS 218 for compliance.

EXHAUST NOISE: Exhaust pipes and mufflers must be in good working order and in constant operation. Straight pipes, gutted pipes, "Hollywood" pipes, glass-packs, and any other type of muffler that makes excessive noise are illegal, according to the Mississippi DMV manual, though the law in place is standard.

EQUIPMENT REQUIREMENTS: Front and rear fenders are required, as is an inspection.

ERRATICS: The state and National Park Service take safe driving on the Natchez Trace Parkway, a popular destination for riders, very seriously. Maximum speed anywhere on the parkway is 50 mph. In many places, it is lower. Be on your guard.

GOOD RESOURCES

Mississippi Department of Public Safety: www.dps.state.ms.us
Mississippi Vehicle Code: www.mscode.com

MISSOURI

RIDEABILITY RANK: 25

With a higher ranking being best for motorcyclists, Missouri ranks 22nd in the nation for population density and 33rd for law enforcement density. Missouri is a river-valley and low-mountains state with rolling hills and fertile flatlands. Roadways tend to be hilly with gentle curves in the flatlands and twisting roads in the Ozarks. The ratio of multi-vehicle motorcycle fatalities to single-vehicle motorcycle fatalities is 51/49. The typical patrol vehicle is a Ford Police Interceptor (Crown Vic) or Chevy Impala. The overall tone of law enforcement toward motorcycle riders is best described as businesslike.

MISSOURI AT A GLANCE

Helmet Law	Yes	Exhaust Noise	No
Eye Protection	Not required	Earphones	Okay
Permit Restrictions	None	Checkpoints	Yes
Insurance	25/50/10	Automated Enforcement	Speed, red light cameras
Reciprocity	Yes		
Handlebar Height Restriction	Yes	School Buses	Yes
Daytime Headlight Use	Not required	Pedestrians	Yes
Left Lane Restriction	None	Move-Over Law	Yes
Unchanging Traffic Signal Law	Yes	Excessive Speed Sanctions	No
Turn Signals	Not required	Mandatory Tow	No
License Plate Display	Yes	HOV	Okay
Fenders	Not required	Feet Down	No
		Erratics	None

For more detailed information on the above, see next page or reference Chapter 2: U.S. Motorcycle Laws and Regulations.

MISSOURI LAWS IN DETAIL

Missouri uses a demerit points system to track moving violations. If you accumulate four points in 12 months, you'll be put on notice. Racking up eight points in 18 months gets you suspended for 30 days. A second suspension for the eight-in-18 is worth 60 days. Third and subsequent suspensions get you 90 days. When you are reinstated after a suspension, your point total is set at four. Driving conviction-free for two years reduces your point total to two. Going without a ticket for three years reduces your points to zero.

If you manage to amass 12 points in a year, 18 points in two years, or 24 points in three years, your driving privileges will be revoked. Driving convictions will remain on your record for at least three years and possibly longer if any of the convictions required a suspension. Major convictions will remain permanently on your record.

A speeding ticket that is in violation of state law is worth three points, while a speeding ticket in violation of a county or municipal ordinance is worth two points. (Whether you are cited under a state or municipal court makes the difference.) Careless and imprudent violations carry two points for a county or municipal violation and four for a state violation. Most other minor violations (excluding DWI, felonies, etc.) are two points. Riding a motorcycle without a proper license is worth two, four, and six points for the first, second, and third offenses, respectively.

HELMET LAW: Helmets that meet specifications of FMVSS 218 are required for all riders and passengers.

HANDLEBAR HEIGHT RESTRICTION: Handlebars can rise to no more than 15 inches above the operator's seat.

UNCHANGING TRAFFIC SIGNAL LAW: In Missouri, motorcyclists have an escape route when faced with a red light that doesn't recognize the motorcycle. Riders may proceed carefully if they have come to a complete stop and waited an unreasonable amount of time and if no other vehicle is approaching the intersection. Note that this law applies only to those stoplights that use sensors to detect motor vehicles. Also note that "unreasonable" is not a precise term—you can still get a ticket for running a red light that you have to fight in court. This law is an "affirmative defense," meaning that you can still get a ticket for it and have to prove yourself in court.

LICENSE PLATE DISPLAY: Plates must be securely fastened, and all parts of the plate must be visible and clean. License plate frames cannot cover any part of the plate.

EQUIPMENT REQUIREMENT: The only requirement is a standard safety inspection. Run what you brung. But plan to have at least one rearview mirror.

GOOD RESOURCES

Missouri Department of Revenue: www.dor.mo.gov
Missouri Revised Statutes: www.moga.mo.gov

MONTANA

RIDEABILITY RANK: 1

With a higher ranking being best for motorcyclists, Montana ranks third in the nation for population density and 12th for law enforcement density. Montana is a rugged grasslands, river, and mountain state with big winds and weather extremes. Roadways tend to be in a constant state of construction. However, because the ratio of multi-vehicle motorcycle fatalities to single-vehicle motorcycle fatalities is 37/63, Montana earns the distinction of being the most rideable state in the nation. The typical patrol vehicle is a Ford Police Interceptor (Crown Vic), Charger, or Chevy Impala. The overall tone of law enforcement toward motorcycle riders is best described as businesslike.

MONTANA AT A GLANCE

Helmet Law	**Partial**	Fenders	**Not required**
Eye Protection	**Not required**	Exhaust Noise	**No**
Permit Restrictions	**Yes**	Earphones	**Okay**
Insurance	**25/50/10, but not required for motorcycles**	Checkpoints	**No**
		Automated Enforcement	**No**
Reciprocity	**Yes**	School Buses	**Yes**
Handlebar Height Restriction	**None**	Pedestrians	**Yes**
Daytime Headlight Use	**Required by law**	Move-Over Law	**Yes**
Left Lane Restriction	**None**	Excessive Speed Sanctions	**No**
Unchanging Traffic Signal Law	**None**	Mandatory Tow	**No**
Turn Signals	**Required by law**	Feet Down	**No**
License Plate Display	**No**	Erratics	**None**

For more detailed information on the above, see next page or reference Chapter 2: U.S. Motorcycle Laws and Regulations.

MONTANA LAWS IN DETAIL

Montana uses a demerit points system to track moving violations. Insurance, racing, and reckless driving carry five points. Speeding is worth three. Most other minor violations are worth two. Conviction points remain on your record for three years, though convictions remain on your record permanently. Multiple traffic tickets don't start putting you in danger of losing your license until you reach 30 points, and then you'll lose it for a good long while.

Three reckless in a period of 12 months will get you suspended for 30 to 365 days. Habitual offenders who earn 30 or more points within a three-year period are awarded a three-year license revocation—including the possibility of a one-year jail sentence and/or an additional fine of $1,000.

Montana is not a member of the Nonresident Violator Compact (NRVC), which is meant to ensure equal treatment of nonresidents and residents and standardize methods for processing citations, as well as the response of the rider/driver to comply to them. This means that if you're nabbed for a moving violation here, the arresting officer is not obligated to release you without posting bond for the fine. If you don't have a method of posting bond (cash works; checks and credit may work), you could end up in jail until you do. And, if you are required to pay the fine or appear in court and fail to do so, your home state will not necessarily suspend your license until you comply with the citation's requirements (pay the fine)—they may never even know about it. States that are not members of this compact are Alaska, California, Michigan, Montana, Oregon, and Wisconsin.

HELMET LAW: Riders under 18 years old are required to wear helmets that conform to FMVSS 218 specifications.

PERMIT RESTRICTIONS: A rider on a motorcycle permit must be under the immediate supervision of a licensed rider.

INSURANCE: Liability insurance is not required for motorcycles in Montana.

TURN SIGNALS: Electric turn signals are required for bikes manufactured in 1953 or later.

EQUIPMENT REQUIREMENTS: A rearview mirror, a passenger seat, footrests, and turn signals are required.

GOOD RESOURCES

Montana Department of Justice: www.doj.mt.gov
Montana State Statutes: http://data.opi.mt.gov/bills/mca_toc/index.htm

NEBRASKA

RIDEABILITY RANK: 9

With a higher ranking being best for motorcyclists, Nebraska ranks eighth in the nation for population density and 20th for law enforcement density. Nebraska is a relatively flat Great Plains state known for farming, ranching, and low hills. Roadways tend to be well maintained. The ratio of multi-vehicle motorcycle fatalities to single-vehicle motorcycle fatalities is 46/54. The typical patrol vehicle is a Ford Police Interceptor (Crown Vic). The overall tone of law enforcement toward motorcycle riders is best described as businesslike.

NEBRASKA AT A GLANCE

Helmet Law	Yes		Exhaust Noise	No
Eye Protection	Not required		Earphones	Okay
Permit Restrictions	Yes		Checkpoints	Yes
Insurance	25/50/25		Automated Enforcement	No
Reciprocity	Yes		School Buses	Yes
Handlebar Height Restriction	Yes		Pedestrians	Yes
Daytime Headlight Use	Not required		Move-Over Law	Yes
Left Lane Restriction	None		Excessive Speed Sanctions	No
Unchanging Traffic Signal Law	None		Mandatory Tow	No
Turn Signals	Not required		Feet Down	No
License Plate Display	No		Erratics	None
Fenders	Required by law			

For more detailed information on the above, see next page or reference Chapter 2: U.S. Motorcycle Laws and Regulations.

NEBRASKA LAWS IN DETAIL

Nebraska uses a demerit points system to track moving violations. Racking up 12 points in a two-year period will get you automatically revoked for six months. This will require you to attend a driver improvement clinic before you can get your license back. If you get your license revoked under the points system twice within five years, you'll lose your license for three years.

Speeding tickets received inside city limits accrue points at a rate of one point for convictions of 5 mph over the limit or less, two points for 5–10 mph over, three points for 10–35 mph over, and four points for 36 mph or greater. Outside city limits, 1–10 mph over will get you one point, 11–15 will get you two points, 15–35 will get you three, and 36 or more will get you four. Other minor traffic violations get you one point. Serious traffic convictions (reckless, willful reckless) get you five or six points. Points will count against you for two years; convictions remain on your record for five.

Completing an approved driver improvement clinic before you hit 12 points can get you a two-point reduction once every five years.

HELMET LAW: All motorcycle operators and passengers are required to wear helmets that meet FMVSS 218 standards.

PERMIT RESTRICTIONS: A rider on a permit must be accompanied by and in visual proximity to a licensed rider 21 years of age or older.

HANDLEBAR HEIGHT RESTRICTION: Motorcycle handgrips can rise to no more than 15 inches above the mounting/fasten point.

EQUIPMENT REQUIREMENTS: Fenders are required front and rear, and a passenger seat and footrests are required to carry a passenger.

GOOD RESOURCES

Nebraska Department of Motor Vehicles: www.dmv.ne.gov
Nebraska State Statutes: http://nebraskalegislature.gov

NEVADA

RIDEABILITY RANK: 32

With a higher ranking being best for motorcyclists, Nevada ranks ninth in the nation for population density and 35th for law enforcement density. Nevada is a Great Basin desert and mountain state with lots of open countryside and beautiful vistas. Roadways tend to be wide-open and mostly straight, but curvy in the mountains. The ratio of multi-vehicle motorcycle fatalities to single-vehicle motorcycle fatalities is 64/36. The typical patrol vehicles are Ford SUVs and Police Interceptors (Crown Vic). The overall tone of law enforcement toward motorcycle riders is best described as businesslike.

NEVADA AT A GLANCE

Helmet Law	Yes	Exhaust Noise	No
Eye Protection	Required by law	Earphones	Okay
Permit Restrictions	Yes	Checkpoints	Yes
Insurance	15/30/10	Automated Enforcement	No
Reciprocity	Yes	School Buses	Yes
Handlebar Height Restriction	Yes	Pedestrians	Yes
Daytime Headlight Use	Not required	Move-Over Law	Yes
Left Lane Restriction	Yes	Excessive Speed Sanctions	No
Unchanging Traffic Signal Law	No	Mandatory Tow	No
Turn Signals	Required by law	HOV	Okay
License Plate Display	No	Feet Down	No
Fenders	Required by law	Erratics	Yes

For more detailed information on the above, see next page or reference Chapter 2: U.S. Motorcycle Laws and Regulations.

NEVADA LAWS IN DETAIL

Nevada uses a demerit points system to track moving violations. If you accumulate 12 points in a year, your license will be suspended. If you have between three and 11 points, you can have three points deducted by completing a driver improvement clinic as often as every year. If you draw lots of attention to yourself via your driving record, it is possible for the state to review your record and introduce additional sanctions.

Speeding 1–10 mph over the limit will cost you one point. Getting nicked for 11–20 over will cost you two. Going 21–30 over is worth three, and 31–40 is worth four. Receiving a conviction for 41 mph over the limit or more will get you five. Driving "too fast for conditions" regardless of speed is worth two points. Reckless and careless driving are worth eight and six points, respectively. Other violations are typically worth four points.

HELMET LAW: All operators and passengers are required to wear helmets that conform to FMVSS 218 standards.

EYE PROTECTION: Glasses, goggles, or a face shield is required unless the motorcycle is equipped with a windshield.

PERMIT RESTRICTIONS: A rider operating under a permit may do so only under the direct visual supervision of a licensed rider on a motorcycle. The supervising rider must be at least 21 years old and must have had a motorcycle license for at least a year. Permitted riders are restricted to daylight hours only, may not carry passengers, and may not drive on limited-access highways and freeways.

HANDLEBAR HEIGHT RESTRICTION: Handgrips may not rise higher than an operator's shoulders while seated.

LEFT LANE RESTRICTION: On highways with three or more lanes, use of the far left lane is prohibited. The center lane is to be used only for passing or turning.

TURN SIGNALS: If your bike was manufactured in 1973 or later, it's required to have turn signals mounted front and rear.

REQUIRED EQUIPMENT: Two mirrors are required, both right and left, and fenders are required front and rear. A passenger seat and footrests are required if carrying a passenger.

ERRATICS: State law specifies that a rider must have one hand on the handlebars at all times.

GOOD RESOURCES

Nevada Department of Motor Vehicles: www.dmvnv.com
Nevada State Statutes: www.leg.state.nv.us

30

NEW HAMPSHIRE

RIDEABILITY RANK: 21

With a higher ranking being best for motorcyclists, New Hampshire ranks 30th in the nation for population density and 19th for law enforcement density. New Hampshire is a picturesque New England state with thick forests and mountains. The ratio of multi-vehicle motorcycle fatalities to single-vehicle motorcycle fatalities is 51/49. The typical patrol vehicle is a Ford Police Interceptor (Crown Vic) or Charger. The overall tone of law enforcement toward motorcycle riders is best described as businesslike.

NEW HAMPSHIRE LAWS IN DETAIL

New Hampshire uses a demerit points system to track moving violations. Adult drivers who accumulate 12 points in a year can get suspended up to three months. If you get 18 points in two years, the suspension can be up to six months. For 24 points in three years, you're looking at up to a year's suspension. Thresholds are lower for younger drivers. Those drivers age 18 to 20 get the same suspensions at nine, 15,

NEW HAMPSHIRE AT A GLANCE

Helmet Law	Partial	Exhaust Noise	Yes
Eye Protection	Required by law	Earphones	Okay
Permit Restrictions	Yes	Checkpoints	Yes
Insurance	25/50/25	Automated Enforcement	No
Reciprocity	Yes	School Buses	Yes
Handlebar Height Restriction	Yes	Pedestrians	Yes
Daytime Headlight Use	Not required	Move-Over Law	Yes
Left Lane Restriction	None	Excessive Speed Sanctions	No
Unchanging Traffic Signal Law	None	Mandatory Tow	No
Turn Signals	Required by law	Feet Down	No
License Plate Display	No	Erratics	Yes
Fenders	Required by law		

For more detailed information on the above, see next page or reference Chapter 2: U.S. Motorcycle Laws and Regulations.

and 21 points (versus 12, 18, and 24) in one, two, and three years, respectively. If you're under 18, the suspensions are the same for six, 12, and 18 points in one, two, and three years, respectively. Habitual offenders (that is, 12 minor convictions in five years; three major convictions such as DWI, reckless, or school bus; or a variety of combinations of major and multiple minor convictions) can get their license revoked for one to four years.

Points range from one to six. Minor offenses cost you one or two, while speeding up to 25 mph over the limit costs you three. Speeding at 25 mph or more over the limit will cost you four. Six-pointers include school bus violations, driving after suspension, racing, reckless, etc. Once every three years, you can earn a three-point deduction by completing a driver improvement clinic.

HELMET LAW: All riders and passengers younger than 18 are required to wear helmets that meet DOT standards.

EYE PROTECTION: Operators must wear glasses, goggles, or a face shield unless the motorcycle is equipped with a windscreen.

PERMIT RESTRICTIONS: Riders on permits cannot carry passengers or drive at night.

INSURANCE: Though recommended, motor vehicles are generally not required to carry liability insurance in New Hampshire. If you're involved in a crash with another vehicle, you are still responsible to pay for the damages you caused. After a crash, DWI, etc., a mandatory minimum liability policy will be required.

HANDLEBAR HEIGHT RESTRICTION: Grips must fall below shoulder height while the rider is seated on the motorcycle.

EXHAUST NOISE: In addition to the usual language about a muffler in good working order and constant operation, the law specifically states that straight pipes are illegal. Fines start at $100. A second offense will cost you $250, while a third offense in a calendar year will set you back $500.

EQUIPMENT REQUIREMENTS: Motorcycles are required to have at least one rearview mirror, fenders front and rear, and a passenger seat, footrests, and handholds if carrying a passenger. Turn signals are required for bikes 1973 and newer. Bikes are also required to have working speedometers and odometers and annual inspections.

ERRATICS: It is against the law at a crosswalk to make a right turn on red when a steady or flashing walk signal is lit, even if there are no pedestrians present. Also, under New Hampshire law, if you hit a dog, you must report it to the dog's owner or a police officer.

GOOD RESOURCES
New Hampshire Division of Motor Vehicles: www.nh.gov
New Hampshire State Statutes: www.gencourt.state.nh.us

31

PART II STATE-BY-STATE

NEW JERSEY

RIDEABILITY RANK: 50

With a higher ranking being best for motorcyclists, New Jersey ranks 50th in the nation for population density and 49th for law enforcement density. New Jersey is a coastal state with some heavy metropolitan areas but also rural hills and woodlands. Roadways tend to be flat and straight, except for the hilly areas in the northwest. And because the ratio of multi-vehicle motorcycle fatalities to single-vehicle motorcycle fatalities is 59/41, New Jersey earns the dubious distinction of being the least rideable state in the nation. The typical patrol vehicle is a Ford Police Interceptor (Crown Vic) with a few SUVs thrown in for good measure. New Jersey law enforcement seems to like the Dodge Durango. The overall tone of law enforcement toward motorcycle riders is best described as businesslike.

NEW JERSEY AT A GLANCE

Helmet Law	Yes	Exhaust Noise	No
Eye Protection	Required by law	Earphones	Okay
Permit Restrictions	Yes	Checkpoints	Yes
Insurance	15/30/5,	Automated Enforcement	Red light cameras
	No-fault optional	School Buses	Yes
Reciprocity	Yes	Pedestrians	Yes
Handlebar Height Restriction	Yes	Move-Over Law	Yes
Daytime Headlight Use	Not required	Excessive Speed Sanctions	Yes
Left Lane Restriction	Yes	Mandatory Tow	Yes
Unchanging Traffic Signal Law	No	HOV	Partial
Turn Signals	Not required	Feet Down	No
License Plate Display	Yes	Erratics	None
Fenders	Not required		

For more detailed information on the above, see next page or reference Chapter 2: U.S. Motorcycle Laws and Regulations.

NEW JERSEY LAWS IN DETAIL

New Jersey uses a demerit points system for tracking moving violations. If you rack up 12 or more points on your license, you'll get suspended. Speeding 1–14 mph over will get you two points, 15–29 will get you four, 30-plus will get you five. Moving violations committed out of state are worth two.

Points in New Jersey are kept on a permanent record, so courts will always be able to review the life history of your driving record. The only way to get them off your current record (and avoid a suspension) is to go a year with no violations or points accrued. This will remove three points from your current record. Taking a defensive driving or driver improvement clinic will reduce your points by two and three points, and you can do this every two to five years depending on the class you take.

But wait, there's more. If you earn six or more points within three years, regardless of whether you've gotten yourself suspended, you'll be awarded a surcharge of $150 plus an additional $25 for every point above six. Other infractions (no insurance, DUI, etc.) also carry automatic surcharges. Also, speeding 20 mph or more doubles the fine.

HELMET LAW: All riders and passengers are required to wear helmets that are FMVSS 218 compliant. The law also states that reflectorization is required on helmets.

EYE PROTECTION: Riders are required to wear goggles or a face shield (glasses/sunglasses don't qualify) unless the motorcycle is equipped with a windscreen.

PERMIT RESTRICTIONS: A rider operating on a permit must be accompanied by a licensed rider from New Jersey who is riding his or her own motorcycle.

HANDLEBAR HEIGHT RESTRICTION: Grips must be below the rider's seated shoulder height.

LEFT LANE RESTRICTION: Drivers are required to keep to the right except to pass another vehicle. "Failure to keep right" will earn you two points if convicted.

TURN SIGNALS: While electric turn signals are not required, you are still required to signal your turns and lane changes. If you have signals on your bike, they have to be in good working order.

LICENSE PLATE DISPLAY: Motorcycle license plates must be clean and visible at all times. They cannot have any numbering or lettering concealed by anything.

EXHAUST NOISE: No vehicle shall emit a sound that is unduly loud or harsh, and each must have a muffler—although what exactly a muffler is hasn't been well defined in New Jersey statutes.

EXCESSIVE SPEED SANCTIONS: Speeding 20 mph or more doubles the fine.

MANDATORY TOW: If you don't have a proper license, if it's suspended or revoked, or if you have no insurance, law enforcement is required to tow your vehicle.

HOV: Some HOV lanes are open to motorcycles, while others are not. HOV lanes and signage will display vehicle eligibility.

EQUIPMENT REQUIREMENTS: Motorcycles are required to have at least one rearview mirror as well as a passenger seat and footrests if carrying a passenger. All equipment must be in working order (self-inspection).

GOOD RESOURCES

New Jersey Motor Vehicle Commission: www.state.nj.us/mvc
Title 39 New Jersey Statutes, Traffic Laws: www.state.mj.us/transportation

NEW MEXICO

RIDEABILITY RANK: 16

With a higher ranking being best for motorcyclists, New Mexico ranks sixth in the nation for population density and 37th for law enforcement density. New Mexico is a sparse-desert, mesa, and forested-mountain state. The ratio of multi-vehicle motorcycle fatalities to single-vehicle motorcycle fatalities is 50/50. The typical patrol vehicles are Ford Police Interceptors (Crown Vics) and SUVs. The overall tone of law enforcement toward motorcycle riders is best described as businesslike.

NEW MEXICO

Helmet Law	**Partial**	Exhaust Noise	**No**
Eye Protection	**Required by law**	Earphones	**Okay**
Permit Restrictions	**Yes**	Checkpoints	**Yes**
Insurance	**25/50/10**	Automated Enforcement	**Speed, red light cameras**
Reciprocity	**Yes**	School Buses	**Yes**
Handlebar Height Restriction	**None**	Pedestrians	**Yes**
Daytime Headlight Use	**Not required**	Move-Over Law	**Yes**
Left Lane Restriction	**None**	Excessive Speed Sanctions	**No**
Unchanging Traffic Signal Law	**None**	Mandatory Tow	**No**
Turn Signals	**Not required**	Feet Down	**No**
License Plate Display	**No**	Erratics	**Yes**
Fenders	**Not required**		

For more detailed information on the above, see next page or reference Chapter 2: U.S. Motorcycle Laws and Regulations.

NEW MEXICO LAWS IN DETAIL

New Mexico uses a demerit points system to track moving violations. If you rack up seven points within a year, the judge who convicts you can recommend that the state suspend your license for up to three months. If you accumulate 12 or more points in a 12-month period, your driver's license will be suspended for a year. Points remain on your record for one year after a conviction.

The way points are assessed in New Mexico is confusing. The law differentiates between speed zones of 15 (school zone), 30 (business district), and 75 mph, but it is not exactly clear what the thresholds are for zones other than those, except that it seems you have to be traveling at 76 mph or more to be awarded demerit points. Points are not awarded for speeding on rural roads two miles or more from city limits—except in Bernalillo County or when a cyclist's (or motorist's) excessive speed was a factor in an accident.

That said, no points appear to be assessed for a conviction of speeding 1–5 mph over the limit. The law does say that speeding 6–15 mph over the limit in a residential (15- or 30-mph) zone or a 75-mph zone is worth three points. Speeding 16–25 mph over the limit in a residential (15- or 30-mph) zone or a 75-mph zone is worth five points. Reckless driving or racing will cost you six points. Getting nicked for 26 mph over the limit in a residential zone or a 75-mph zone is worth eight points. Most other moving violations (careless, failure to obey, etc.) carry the weight of two or three points.

HELMET LAW: Riders and passengers under 18 years of age are required to wear helmets that meet FMVSS 218 standards.

EYE PROTECTION: Glasses, goggles, or a face shield is required by law unless the motorcycle is equipped with a windscreen.

PERMIT RESTRICTIONS: Riders operating under permits are forbidden to carry passengers. A permitted rider must be accompanied by a licensed driver 21 or older who has had a license for at least three years.

EQUIPMENT REQUIREMENTS: Motorcycles are required to have at least one rearview mirror, two brakes, and a passenger seat and footrests if carrying a passenger. They are subject to random inspections.

ERRATICS: Motorcycle maneuverability: A bike that can't make a 90-degree turn within a 14-foot circle is considered an "unsafe vehicle," so be wary of riding an elongated custom bike. Police officers can require you to demonstrate that your bike can make this turn. If you can't make your bike do it, it's possible you'll receive a misdemeanor charge and have your bike towed and impounded.

GOOD RESOURCES

New Mexico Motor Vehicle Division: www.mvd.newmexico.gov
New Mexico State Statutes: www.nmlegis.gov/lcs/statutes.aspx

NEW YORK

RIDEABILITY RANK: 49

With a higher ranking being best for motorcyclists, New York ranks 43rd in the nation for population density and 48th for law enforcement density. Upstate New York is very scenic, but "downstate" is home to some of the most congested, trafficked roads in the country. The ratio of multi-vehicle motorcycle fatalities to single-vehicle motorcycle fatalities is 59/41. New York is known as a state notorious for writing traffic tickets and is one of the few states that conduct motorcycle-specific checkpoints. The typical patrol vehicle is a Ford Police Interceptor (Crown Vic) or a Chevy Tahoe, with a few Dodge Chargers and Harley-Davidsons thrown in. The overall tone of law enforcement toward motorcycle riders is best described as businesslike.

NEW YORK AT A GLANCE

Helmet Law	Yes	Exhaust Noise	Yes
Eye Protection	Required by law	Earphones	One ear only
Permit Restrictions	Yes	Checkpoints	Yes
Insurance	25/50/10, No-fault	Automated Enforcement	Red light cameras
		School Buses	Yes
Reciprocity	Yes	Pedestrians	Yes
Handlebar Height Restriction	Yes	Move-Over Law	No
Daytime Headlight Use	Required by law	Excessive Speed Sanctions	Yes
Left Lane Restriction	Yes	Mandatory Tow	No
Unchanging Traffic Signal Law	No	HOV	Okay
Turn Signals	Required by law	Feet Down	No
License Plate Display	Yes	Erratics	Yes
Fenders	Not required		

For more detailed information on the above, see next page or reference Chapter 2: U.S. Motorcycle Laws and Regulations.

NEW YORK LAWS IN DETAIL

New York is a state that uses a demerit points system, but some infractions or combinations of infractions ("persistent violators") will accelerate the suspension/revocation process. For example, three speeding or misdemeanor tickets within 18 months, three school bus violations in three years, one leaving the scene of an injury or fatal accident, or one "participating in a speeding contest" will get your license revoked for at least six months. Two speeding contests within 12 months will get your license revoked for a year or more.

Points on your record are based on the date you commit the violation. Generally, racking up 11 points or more within 18 months will get your license suspended. Speeding up to 10 mph over and most minor traffic offenses will cost you three points. Speeding 11–20 over, having "inadequate brakes," or tailgating will cost you four points. Reckless riding or a school bus violation will net you five points. Speeding 21–30 over is worth six, 31–40 is worth eight, and more than 40 is worth 11 points. It's safe to say that a 100+ speeding ticket will get you an instant suspension.

You can reduce your total by up to four points by taking an approved defensive driving course. However, completion of a course cannot prevent a mandatory suspension or revocation, cannot be applied as a "credit" against future points, and cannot prevent a mandatory driver assessment.

HELMET LAW: All riders and passengers must wear DOT-compliant helmets.

EYE PROTECTION: Goggles or a face shield is required. Regular eyeglasses or sunglasses may not cut it for eye protection, as eyewear used for eye protection must meet national standards (ANSI Z87.1) for compliance. Windshields don't count for anything.

PERMIT RESTRICTIONS: There are few restrictions for a rider operating on an instruction permit, the exception being that a rider must have a supervising driver with a valid motorcycle license who is at least 21 years old within a quarter mile of the learner at all times. If you're visiting from another state on a permit, you must also obey the restrictions of your home-state permit if you're younger than 18.

HANDLEBAR HEIGHT RESTRICTION: Handlebars or grips may not be more than the height of the operator's shoulders.

LEFT LANE RESTRICTION: On state roads, the left lane is for passing only, but reports suggest that like everywhere else in the country, this law is not really enforced.

TURN SIGNALS: Turn signals are required if the motorcycle was originally equipped or is 1985 or newer. Regardless, signaling is required: Riders must signal their intention to turn 100 feet or more in advance.

LICENSE PLATE DISPLAY: Must face the rear and be visible for at least 50 feet.

EXHAUST NOISE: The exhaust pipe regulations in New York lean heavily toward OEM only. The law specifies that the baffles have to be intact (no straight pipes). Also, the bike can have no modifications that raise the noise level above that at which it came originally from the factory.

CHECKPOINTS: Not only do New York officers conduct checkpoints, they actually conduct motorcycle-specific checkpoints.

EXCESSIVE SPEED SANCTIONS: There are too many to list, but here are some examples: If you get two speeding summons in a work zone, your license will be suspended. A speed contest is a crime rather than a traffic violation. And it is possible to get a 15-day jail sentence for 11 mph over the limit.

EQUIPMENT REQUIREMENTS: At least one rearview mirror is mandatory, and a passenger seat is required if you're carrying a passenger.

ERRATICS: Be careful in the city: Right and left turns on red are not permitted in New York City and some surrounding areas. Brakes on 1971 and newer motorcycles are required on both wheels. New York assigns four demerit points for "inadequate brakes." This nebulous term is probably not intended specifically for motorcycles, but it's logical to assume that a bike with only one brake, front or rear, would be in violation.

If you're issued a ticket for a noncriminal moving violation in New York City, Buffalo, Rochester, or certain areas of Suffolk County (Babylon, Brookhaven, Huntington, Islip, and Smithtown), your process will not be handled by the usual county courts but by the New York DMV Traffic Violations Bureau (TVB). Good sources warn that you do *not* want to get a citation in one of these burghs, as they are much more difficult to fight.

GOOD RESOURCES
Motorcycle Manual: www.nydmv.state.ny.us/mcmanual/mcmanual.htm
Vehicle & Traffic Law: http://public.leginfo.state.ny.us/menuf.cgi

NORTH CAROLINA

RIDEABILITY RANK: 46

With a higher ranking being best for motorcyclists, North Carolina ranks 35th in the nation for population density and 34th for law enforcement density. North Carolina is a southern state with great beaches, farmland, woodlands, and mountains. Rural roadways tend to be narrow and curving, while major highways are wide and flat. The ratio of multi-vehicle motorcycle fatalities to single-vehicle motorcycle fatalities is 55/45. North Carolina is known informally as a state notorious for writing traffic tickets. The typical patrol vehicle is a Ford Police Interceptor (Crown Vic) or Charger. The overall tone of law enforcement toward motorcycle riders is best described as businesslike.

NORTH CAROLINA AT A GLANCE

Helmet Law	Yes	Exhaust Noise	No
Eye Protection	Not required	Earphones	Okay
Permit Restrictions	Yes	Checkpoints	Yes
Insurance	30/60/25	Automated Enforcement	Red light cameras
Reciprocity	Yes	School Buses	Yes
Handlebar Height Restriction	None	Pedestrians	Yes
Daytime Headlight Use	Required by law	Move-Over Law	Yes
Left Lane Restriction	No	Excessive Speed Sanctions	No
Unchanging Traffic Signal Law	Yes	Mandatory Tow	No
Turn Signals	Not required	Feet Down	No
License Plate Display	Yes	Erratics	None
Fenders	Not required		

For more detailed information on the above, see next page or reference Chapter 2: U.S. Motorcycle Laws and Regulations.

NORTH CAROLINA LAWS IN DETAIL

North Carolina uses a demerit points system to track moving violations. Once you accumulate seven points, plan to attend a driver improvement clinic, which will drop your point total by three. If you rack up 12 points within three years, you're eligible for a 60-day suspension. Getting eight more points within three years of a suspension will get you suspended again, for six months. A third suspension is good for a year.

Speeding tickets are generally worth three points. Major violations are three to five points, and minor violations are two points. However, at speeds higher than 55 mph, North Carolina gets tough. Any speeding conviction over 75 mph can get you suspended. Two speeding tickets at any speed over 55 mph within 12 months can get you suspended. A ticket for speeding over 55 and a reckless within a year can get you suspended. Anything more than 15 over at speeds of 55 or greater will get you revoked for 30 days. A second conviction like this in a year gets you revoked for 60 days, as does racing (three-year suspension and seizure!) or any combination of speeding and reckless. Two reckless convictions in a year will get you a one-year suspension.

HELMET LAW: All riders must wear helmets that comply with FMVSS 218. Be aware that law enforcement officers in North Carolina have been well trained in identifying noncompliant helmets and are quite enthusiastic about enforcing the law.

PERMIT RESTRICTIONS: A rider on a permit cannot carry passengers.

UNCHANGING TRAFFIC SIGNAL LAW: North Carolina offers an affirmative defense for violations of a signal light that does not recognize the motorcycle: You must bring the motorcycle to a complete stop; no other vehicle with the right of way is in or approaching the intersection; no pedestrians are attempting to cross; and you wait a minimum of three minutes. You can still get nicked for this and have to appear in court. But if you can demonstrate that you met these criteria, you can have your citation dismissed.

LICENSE PLATE DISPLAY: The license plate is required to be mounted on the rear, horizontal and upright, and free of dust and dirt (legible). It cannot be bent or mutilated, and no part of it can be hidden in any way.

EQUIPMENT REQUIREMENTS: Motorcycles are required to sport a rearview mirror, a working speedometer, and a passenger seat and footrests if the rider is carrying a passenger. Also, they must pass an annual inspection.

GOOD RESOURCES

North Carolina Statutes Chapter 20: www.ncga.state.nc.us

Department of Transportation Division of Motor Vehicles: www.ncdot.org/dmv

NORTH DAKOTA

RIDEABILITY RANK: 2

With a higher ranking being best for motorcyclists, North Dakota ranks fourth in the nation for population density and 13th for law enforcement density. North Dakota is a plains state famous for its Badlands and Red River Valley areas. Roadways tend to be flat and straight. The ratio of multi-vehicle motorcycle fatalities to single-vehicle motorcycle fatalities is 41/59. The typical patrol vehicle is a Ford Police Interceptor (Crown Vic). The overall tone of law enforcement toward motorcycle riders is best described as businesslike.

NORTH DAKOTA AT A GLANCE

Helmet Law	Partial	Fenders	Yes
Eye Protection	Not required	Exhaust Noise	No
Permit Restrictions	Yes	Earphones	Okay
Insurance	20/50/25, No-fault	Checkpoints	Yes
		Automated Enforcement	No
Reciprocity	Yes	School Buses	Yes
Handlebar Height Restriction	Yes	Pedestrians	Yes
Daytime Headlight Use	Not required	Move-Over Law	Yes
Left Lane Restriction	No	Excessive Speed Sanctions	No
Unchanging Traffic Signal Law	No	Mandatory Tow	No
Turn Signals	Required by law	Feet Down	No
License Plate Display	Yes	Erratics	None

For more detailed information on the above, see next page or reference Chapter 2: U.S. Motorcycle Laws and Regulations.

NORTH DAKOTA LAWS IN DETAIL

North Dakota uses a demerit points system for moving violations. Racking up 12 points will get you suspended for seven days, and every point greater than 11 will get you seven days. On roads marked less than 70 mph, 1–10 mph over the limit won't cost you any points, and point attributions are minimal until you exceed 26 mph over (nine points). Going 46 over will earn you 15 points. On roads marked 70 or greater, most point costs are the same, but penalties for 21–30 over are a little more severe.

Points drop off your record at a rate of one every three months of conviction-free driving. You can remove three points from your record by completing an approved driver improvement clinic. You can also take a driver improvement clinic in lieu of points for any violation assessed five or fewer points. You can do this once every 12 months, although it is not valid when combined with other offers.

HELMET LAW: Operators and passengers under 18 are required to wear DOT-compliant helmets. Passengers of a rider who is required to wear a helmet must also wear a helmet no matter what age.

PERMIT RESTRICTION: Riders on instruction permits can ride during the daytime only, and they cannot carry passengers.

HANDLEBAR HEIGHT RESTRICTION: Handgrips must be below shoulder height.

TURN SIGNALS: Electric turn signals are required by law for bikes 1976 and newer.

LICENSE PLATE DISPLAY: Plates must be mounted on the rear of the motorcycle, conspicuously displayed, horizontal, and illuminated.

EQUIPMENT REQUIREMENTS: Motorcycles are required to have a rearview mirror, fenders front and rear, a passenger seat and footrests if carrying a passenger, and a working speedometer and odometer.

ERRATICS: If an emergency vehicle is parked at the scene of a crash with lights flashing, you must pull over to the right and stop before continuing at your own risk.

GOOD RESOURCES

Vehicle Code: www.legis.nd.gov/cencode/t39.html
Rules and Regulations: www.dot.nd.gov

OHIO

RIDEABILITY RANK: 30

With a higher ranking being best for motorcyclists, Ohio ranks 42nd in the nation for population density and 22nd for law enforcement density. Ohio is an industrious Great Lakes state with crowded highways but also scenic, rural, rugged hills and forests. Roadways tend to be well marked and maintained. The ratio of multi-vehicle motorcycle fatalities to single-vehicle motorcycle fatalities is 51/49. Ohio is known informally as being notorious for writing traffic tickets. The typical patrol vehicle is a Ford Police Interceptor (Crown Vic), Chevy Impala, or Dodge Charger. There are many police motorcycles, including Harley-Davidsons, BMWs, and Kawasakis. Traffic enforcement vehicles must have flashing lights and identification printed on the vehicle. The overall tone of law enforcement toward motorcycle riders is best described as businesslike.

OHIO AT A GLANCE

Helmet Law	Partial	Exhaust Noise	No
Eye Protection	Required by law	Earphones	One ear only
Permit Restrictions	Yes	Checkpoints	Yes
Insurance	12.5/25/7.5	Automated Enforcement	Speed, red light cameras
Reciprocity	Yes		
Handlebar Height Restriction	Yes	School Buses	Yes
Daytime Headlight Use	Not required	Pedestrians	Yes
Left Lane Restriction	Yes	Move-Over Law	Yes
Unchanging Traffic Signal Law	No	Excessive Speed Sanctions	No
Turn Signals	Required by law	Mandatory Tow	No
License Plate Display	No	HOV	Okay
Fenders	Not required	Feet Down	No
		Erratics	None

For more detailed information on the above, see next page or reference Chapter 2: U.S. Motorcycle Laws and Regulations.

OHIO LAWS IN DETAIL

Ohio is a state that uses a demerit points system. All moving violations and some speed violations are two points. Willful or wanton disregard for safety will earn you four points. Six-point violations include fleeing, leaving the scene of a crash, racing, operating under suspension or revocation, and various high-level violations such as DWI, vehicular homicide, etc.

A speeding violation will net you zero to four points, depending on the speed limit you violated and by how much. Exceeding any speed limit by 30 mph or more will cost you four points. At 55 mph or greater, more than 10 over but less than 30 is worth two points. At less than 55 mph, more than 5 but less than 30 will get you two points. Anything less results in no demerit points. You can win back two points by completing an approved defensive driving course.

A driver who has accumulated six points in a two-year period will receive a warning letter. If you rack up 12 or more points in a two-year period, expect to have your driving privileges suspended for six months. Additionally, you'll have to file proof of insurance for the next three to five years. You'll also have to take a defensive driving course and retake the complete driver exam to get your license reinstated.

HELMET LAW: Operators and passengers under 18 are required to wear DOT-compliant helmets. Novice operators and their passengers, regardless of age, are required to wear helmets. A novice is defined as having a motorcycle license for one year or less. All motorcycle passengers, regardless of age, are required to wear helmets when they are riding with an operator who is required to wear a helmet.

EYE PROTECTION: Riders and passengers must use eye protection— glasses, goggles, or a windshield.

PERMIT RESTRICTIONS: Riders on permits are restricted to daylight riding only. They may not carry passengers, and they may not use congested roadways or interstate highways. Permitted riders must wear helmets.

HANDLEBAR HEIGHT RESTRICTION: Handlebars can rise to no more than 15 inches above the operator's seat.

LEFT LANE RESTRICTION: Drive on the right half of the roadway except during the following situations: when overtaking, on a road with three or more marked lanes, on a one-way street, when directed by a police officer or traffic control device, or when an obstruction makes it necessary for you to drive left-of-center.

EARPHONES: Headphones or earphones are limited to one ear only. However, speakers mounted inside the helmet are okay.

EQUIPMENT REQUIREMENTS: Motorcycles are required to have at least one rearview mirror right or left and a passenger seat and footpegs if carrying a passenger. A random inspection at the roadside is not uncommon.

GOOD RESOURCES

Ohio Motorcycle Manual: www.publicsafety.ohio.gov/links/mop0001.pdf
Ohio Motor Vehicle Laws: www.publicsafety.ohio.gov/links/hsy7607.pdf

OKLAHOMA

RIDEABILITY RANK: 23

With a higher ranking being best for motorcyclists, Oklahoma ranks 14th in the nation for population density and 23rd for law enforcement density. Oklahoma is a high-plain to low-wetland state with low mountains, prairies, and arid grasslands. The ratio of multi-vehicle motorcycle fatalities to single-vehicle motorcycle fatalities is 58/42. The typical patrol vehicle is a Dodge Charger or Ford Police Interceptor (Crown Vic). At one time, the state police even had a Suzuki Hayabusa 1300. The overall tone of law enforcement toward motorcycle riders is best described as businesslike.

OKLAHOMA LAWS IN DETAIL

Oklahoma uses a demerit points system to track moving violations. Racking up 10 points within five years will get you suspended. You may be given an option to attend a driver improvement clinic to avoid getting your license suspended or revoked. Two points are deducted from your record for every year you remain conviction-free. Your

OKLAHOMA AT A GLANCE

Helmet Law	Partial	Exhaust Noise	No
Eye Protection	Required by law	Earphones	Okay
Permit Restrictions	Yes	Checkpoints	Yes
Insurance	10/20/10	Automated Enforcement	No
Reciprocity	Yes	School Buses	Yes
Handlebar Height Restriction	Yes	Pedestrians	Yes
Daytime Headlight Use	Required by law	Move-Over Law	Yes
Left Lane Restriction	Yes!	Excessive Speed Sanctions	No
Unchanging Traffic Signal Law	Yes!	Mandatory Tow	No
Turn Signals	Required by law	Feet Down	No
License Plate Display	No	Erratics	No
Fenders	Required by law		

For more detailed information on the above, see next page or reference Chapter 2: U.S. Motorcycle Laws and Regulations.

points are reduced to zero if you go three years without a traffic violation conviction. Once every two years, you can complete a driver improvement clinic to have two points removed from your record.

A speeding ticket costs you two points. Speeding at 25 mph or more above the limit costs you three. Reckless driving is worth four, as is a school bus violation. Most other violations are in the one- to two-point range. In Oklahoma, speeding tickets 10 mph over or less are not awarded any points.

HELMET LAW: Helmets meeting FMVSS 218 requirements are mandatory for riders and passengers younger than 18.

EYE PROTECTION: Glasses, goggles, or a face shield is required by law unless the bike has a windshield.

PERMIT RESTRICTIONS: Permit restrictions apply only to riders younger than 16. Maximum displacement is 250 cc, no passengers are allowed, and you may only ride between 5 a.m. and 10 p.m. If your motorcycle is less than 150 cc, you cannot exceed 35 mph. If it's between 150 and 250 cc, you can travel at the posted limit but not on any high-speed road with a posted minimum speed limit (interstate or turnpike). When riding on a permit, you must be within visual contact of your "instructor," meaning an adult 21 or older with an Oklahoma driver's license with a motorcycle endorsement.

HANDLEBAR HEIGHT RESTRICTION: Handlebars can rise no higher than the operator's eye level when he or she is seated on the bike.

LEFT LANE RESTRICTION: All drivers are required to travel in the right lane only, except to pass or turn left. The cost of a ticket for using the left lane illegally is the minimum ticket you can get: $190. Woohoo!

UNCHANGING TRAFFIC SIGNAL LAW: Motorcyclists are allowed to proceed through an unchanging red traffic signal if the signal fails to recognize the motorcycle. The following conditions must be met: the rider must have come to a complete stop and there are no other vehicles approaching the intersection, or those approaching are too far away to pose a safety hazard. Note that this law only applies to traffic control devices that use sensors; for timed lights, riders must wait until they change.

TURN SIGNALS: Electric turn signals are required by law if your bike is a 2005 model or newer.

EQUIPMENT REQUIREMENTS: Rearview mirrors left and right are required, as are fenders front and rear, a passenger seat and footrests if carrying a passenger, and turn signals for 2005 and newer bikes. A working speedometer and an inspection are also required.

GOOD RESOURCES

Oklahoma Department of Public Safety: www.dps.state.ok.us
Oklahoma State Statutes: www.oklegislature.gov

OREGON

RIDEABILITY RANK: 3

With a higher ranking being best for motorcyclists, Oregon ranks 12th in the nation for population density and 2nd for law enforcement density. Oregon is a coastal-mountain, fertile-valley, and high-desert state. Roadways tend to be well maintained, scenic, and twisty in the mountains. The ratio of multi-vehicle motorcycle fatalities to single-vehicle motorcycle fatalities is 48/52. The typical patrol vehicle is a Ford Police Interceptor (Crown Vic); an SUV or pickup, marked or unmarked, is not uncommon. The overall tone of law enforcement toward motorcycle riders is best described as businesslike.

OREGON LAWS IN DETAIL
The state of Oregon does not use a demerit points system to track moving violations. Three convictions, three accidents, or any combination in 18 months will get you "restricted" for 30 days if you're 18 or older. The restriction is that you cannot drive

OREGON AT A GLANCE

Helmet Law	Yes	Exhaust Noise	Yes
Eye Protection	Not required	Earphones	Okay
Permit Restrictions	Yes	Checkpoints	No
Insurance	25/50/10	Automated Enforcement	Speed, red light cameras
Reciprocity	Yes	School Buses	Yes
Handlebar Height Restriction	None	Pedestrians	Yes
Daytime Headlight Use	Required by law	Move-Over Law	Yes
Left Lane Restriction	Clearly Not	Excessive Speed Sanctions	Yes
Unchanging Traffic Signal Law	No	Mandatory Tow	No
Turn Signals	Required by law	HOV	Okay
License Plate Display	Yes	Feet Down	No
Fenders	Required by law	Erratics	None

For more detailed information on the above, see next page or reference Chapter 2: U.S. Motorcycle Laws and Regulations.

between midnight and 5 A.M. unless it's job related. Four accidents, four convictions, or any combination in two years will get your license suspended for 30 days. If you're under 18, restrictions happen sooner and penalties get worse.

Habitual offenders are often required to participate in a driver improvement clinic, even for infractions as simple as speeding, running a red light, and failure to signal a lane change. Your license can be revoked for five years if you are convicted of three or more traffic crimes (really bad stuff including reckless, fleeing, etc.) or 20 or more traffic violations within a five-year period.

Oregon is not a member of the Nonresident Violator Compact (NRVC), which is meant to ensure equal treatment of nonresidents and resident, and standardize methods for processing citations, as well as the response of the rider/driver to comply to them. This means that if you're nabbed for a moving violation here, the arresting officer is not obligated to release you without posting bond for the fine. If you don't have a method of posting bond (cash works; checks and credit may work), you could end up in jail until you do. If you are required to pay the fine or appear in court and fail to do so, your home state will not necessarily suspend your license until you comply with the citation's requirements (pay the fine)—they may never even know about it. States that are not members of this compact are Alaska, California, Michigan, Montana, Oregon, and Wisconsin.

HELMET LAW: All riders and passengers are required to wear FMVSS 218 helmets.

PERMIT RESTRICTIONS: Riders on permits can ride only during daylight hours and cannot carry passengers. They must also be supervised by a licensed rider who is 21 or older and uses a separate vehicle.

TURN SIGNALS: Required for bikes manufactured after 1972. Whether a motorcycle has signals on it or not, the operator is required by law to signal turns and lane changes.

LICENSE PLATE DISPLAY: Any cover used on a plate cannot render it unreadable or alter the plate's appearance (even a clear cover can affect the plate's reflectivity).

EXHAUST NOISE: It is prohibited to use an exhaust system or component identified for "competition use only" on any property. The only exception would be a motor sports facility in a practice session or racing event.

EXCESSIVE SPEED SANCTIONS: Speeding tickets, even minor write-ups, are expensive in Oregon. Getting nicked at 30 over, but less than 100 mph, can run you $350 to $700. Being awarded a ticket for 100+ carries a base fine of $1,148.

REQUIRED EQUIPMENT: Bikes are required to carry fenders front and rear, at least one mirror, and a passenger seat and footrests (if carrying a passenger). Random inspections are conducted, so you need to have your affairs in order.

GOOD RESOURCES
Oregon Driver and Motor Vehicles: www.oregondmv.com
Oregon Vehicle Code Book: www.oregon.gov

PENNSYLVANIA

RIDEABILITY RANK: 29

With a higher ranking being best for motorcyclists, Pennsylvania ranks 41st in the nation for population density and 18th for law enforcement density. Pennsylvania is an industrial and agricultural mountain state. Roadways tend to be scenic and challenging. The ratio of multi-vehicle motorcycle fatalities to single-vehicle motorcycle fatalities is 54/46. Pennsylvania is known informally as a state notorious for writing traffic tickets. There is no typical patrol vehicle, though there are a lot of Ford Police Interceptors (Crown Vics), SUVs, Chevy Impalas, and Harley-Davidsons. The overall tone of law enforcement toward motorcycle riders is best described as businesslike.

PENNSYLVANIA LAWS IN DETAIL

Pennsylvania uses a points system to track moving violations. If you accrue six points, you are required to take a special written test. Achieving six points a second time gets you an administrative hearing. Every time you run it up past six after that gets you either another hearing or a suspension.

PENNSYLVANIA AT A GLANCE

Helmet Law	Partial		Exhaust Noise	No
Eye Protection	Required by law		Earphones	Prohibited
Permit Restrictions	Yes		Checkpoints	Yes
Insurance	15/30/5, No-fault optional		Automated Enforcement	Red light cameras
			School Buses	Yes
Reciprocity	Yes		Pedestrians	Yes
Handlebar Height Restriction	None		Move-Over Law	Yes
Daytime Headlight Use	Required by law		Excessive Speed Sanctions	Yes
Left Lane Restriction	No		Mandatory Tow	Yes
Unchanging Traffic Signal Law	No		HOV	Okay
Turn Signals	Not required		Feet Down	No
License Plate Display	Yes		Erratics	None
Fenders	Required by law			

For more detailed information on the above, see next page or reference Chapter 2: U.S. Motorcycle Laws and Regulations.

Drivers younger than 18 get a 90-day suspension right away for six points or for being convicted of driving 26 mph over the limit. Second-timers get a 120-day suspension. Reckless driving, fleeing, school bus violations, etc., will get you suspended or revoked right away at any age.

Once you reach 11 points, your license will be automatically suspended. If it's your first suspension, you get five days per point on your record. Your second suspension gets you 10 days per point. A third suspension gets you 15 days per point, and any further suspensions last one year.

Typical moving violations are two to four points. Speeding 6–10 over will get you two; 11–15 will get you three; 16–25 will get you four; 26 on up will get you five. Any of these infractions committed in a highway work zone also include a 15-day suspension. Speeding at 31 mph or more over the limit will also get you an administrative hearing for an examination of your driving record. This will result in a 15-day suspension and/or an on-road retest of your driving abilities. Skipping this hearing will get you a 60-day suspension.

Demonstrating safe driving behavior—going 12 months without a violation—knocks three points off your record. If your record gets down to zero and stays that way for a year, further convictions are started over as the first accumulation of points.

HELMET LAW: Riders younger than 21 are required to wear helmets that meet FMVSS 218 standards. Riders 21 and older who have A) either two full calendar years of motorcycle licensure or B) completed a state-approved motorcycle training course (MSF) can choose whether or not to wear a helmet. Passengers 21 years of age or older are not required to wear helmets if the operator they're riding with isn't required to wear one.

EYE PROTECTION: Glasses, goggles, or a face shield is required by law.

PERMIT RESTRICTIONS: Riders on a permit cannot carry passengers (other than an instructor) or ride at night. A permitted rider must wear a helmet and eye protection.

DAYTIME HEADLIGHT USE: Using headlights in the daytime is required by law for bikes 1973 and newer.

LICENSE PLATE DISPLAY: Plates must be clearly visible, in a horizontal position, not less than 12 inches from the ground, and mounted in a way that prevents the plate from swinging.

EARPHONES: Using headphones or earphones is prohibited unless it's for a communication device (intercom, for example).

EXCESSIVE SPEED SANCTIONS: Speeding at 31 mph or more over the limit will also get you an administrative hearing for an examination of your driving record, and it will result in a 15-day suspension and/or an on-road retest of your driving abilities. Skipping this hearing will get you a 60-day suspension.

EQUIPMENT REQUIREMENTS: Bikes are required to have a rearview mirror; front and rear fenders; a passenger seat, footrests, and handholds if carrying a passenger; a working speedometer and odometer if originally equipped; and an annual inspection.

GOOD RESOURCE
Pennsylvania Vehicle Code and Driver and Vehicle Services: www.dmv.state.pa.us

RHODE ISLAND

RIDEABILITY RANK: 42

With a higher ranking being best for motorcyclists, Rhode Island ranks 49th in the nation for population density and 44th for law enforcement density. Rhode Island is a surprisingly diverse, tiny state. Roadways tend to be well maintained, narrow, and curvy. The ratio of multi-vehicle motorcycle fatalities to single-vehicle motorcycle fatalities is 49/51. The typical patrol vehicle is a Ford Police Interceptor (Crown Vic) or Chevy Impala. The overall tone of law enforcement toward motorcycle riders is best described as businesslike, although it borders on enthusiastic in some jurisdictions.

RHODE ISLAND LAWS IN DETAIL

Rhode Island does not use a demerit points system to track moving violations. Anyone convicted of four moving violations—speeding or other common infractions—within 18 months may have to endure additional fines up to $1,000, 60 hours of driver

RHODE ISLAND AT A GLANCE

Helmet Law	Partial	Exhaust Noise	Yes
Eye Protection	Required by law	Earphones	Prohibited by law
Permit Restrictions	Yes	Checkpoints	No
Insurance	25/50/25	Automated Enforcement	Red light cameras
Reciprocity	Not really	School Buses	Yes
Handlebar Height Restriction	Yes	Pedestrians	Yes
Daytime Headlight Use	Not required	Move-Over Law	Yes
Left Lane Restriction	Yes	Excessive Speed Sanctions	Yes
Unchanging Traffic Signal Law	No	Mandatory Tow	No
Turn Signals	Not required	Feet Down	No
License Plate Display	No	Erratics	Yes
Fenders	Required by law, front and rear		

For more detailed information on the above, see next page or reference Chapter 2: U.S. Motorcycle Laws and Regulations.

improvement clinics, 60 hours of community service, and a suspension or revocation of their license up to one to two years. Speeding 25 mph or more over the limit can be considered reckless driving. Rhode Island isn't messing around with habitual violators.

HELMET LAW: All passengers are required to wear helmets, regardless of age. Riders under 21 are required to wear helmets, and all riders regardless of age are required to wear helmets for one year after first obtaining their motorcycle endorsement.

EYE PROTECTION: Glasses, goggles, or a face shield is required for all operators.

PERMIT RESTRICTIONS: A rider on a permit cannot carry passengers and must be under the direct supervision of a licensed operator 18 or older.

RECIPROCITY: Rhode Island does have reciprocity with other states, but it does not actively request from or inform other states of moving violations (except for Massachusetts).

HANDLEBAR HEIGHT RESTRICTION: Handlebars can rise to no more than 15 inches above the operator's seat. Apparently, years ago, there was a rather enthusiastic police officer who carried a tape measure and protractor for the purpose of measuring handlebar height and fork angles.

LEFT LANE RESTRICTION: Drivers are required to remain in the left lane except for passing and emergencies, but this law is rarely enforced.

EXHAUST NOISE: There are local ordinances in place that apply to motorcycles and car stereos. The state law specifies that you can run no more than 86 decibels in speed zones 35 mph or less, and no more than 90 decibels above those speeds.

EXCESSIVE SPEED SANCTIONS: Speeding tickets 10 and under are $85. Anything greater than that costs you $10 per mile per hour with a minimum fine of $195. Everything else you can think of is $75.

EQUIPMENT REQUIREMENTS: Motorcycles are required to have a left-side rearview mirror and fenders front and rear. A passenger seat, footrests, and handholds are required to carry a passenger. The motorcycle is also required to have a working speedometer if it was originally equipped with one. You should also plan to submit to a bike inspection.

ERRATICS: Stunt riding is not tolerated well in Rhode Island. Speeding 25+ can be charged as reckless. Reckless through showboating, wheelies, or stoppies can get you impounded on the spot if the officer sees you do it. Racing is serious business. It includes, for a first offense, jail time of up to a year, fines from $500 to $1,000, and community service.

GOOD RESOURCES
Rhode Island General Laws: www.rilin.state.ri.us/Statutes/
Rhode Island Division of Motor Vehicles: www.dmv.ri.gov

41

SOUTH CAROLINA

RIDEABILITY RANK: 38

With a higher ranking being best for motorcyclists, South Carolina ranks 29th in the nation for population density and 36th for law enforcement density. South Carolina is a Deep South state with coastal plains, rolling hills, and low mountains. The ratio of multi-vehicle motorcycle fatalities to single-vehicle motorcycle fatalities is 56/44. The typical patrol vehicle is a Ford Police Interceptor (Crown Vic), Charger, or Chevy Impala. The overall tone of law enforcement toward motorcycle riders is best described as businesslike.

SOUTH CAROLINA AT A GLANCE

Helmet Law	Partial	Exhaust Noise	No
Eye Protection	Required by law	Earphones	Okay
Permit Restrictions	Yes	Checkpoints	Yes
Insurance	15/30/10	Automated Enforcement	No
Reciprocity	Yes	School Buses	Yes
Handlebar Height Restriction	None	Pedestrians	Yes
Daytime Headlight Use	Required by law	Move-Over Law	Yes
Left Lane Restriction	None	Excessive Speed Sanctions	No
Unchanging Traffic Signal Law	Yes	Mandatory Tow	No
Turn Signals	Not required	Feet Down	No
License Plate Display	Yes	Erratics	None
Fenders	Not required		

For more detailed information on the above, see next page or reference Chapter 2: U.S. Motorcycle Laws and Regulations.

SOUTH CAROLINA LAWS IN DETAIL

South Carolina uses a demerit points system to track moving violations. If you accumulate 12 points (six points for restricted licenses, learner's permits, and conditional/provisional licenses), your license will be suspended. Points are reduced by half after a year of conviction-free driving, and they are dropped from your record after two. Convictions, however, remain on your record for three years. You can knock four points off your record by completing a driver improvement clinic once every three years.

Most typical moving violations cost you four points. Speeding at 10 mph over or less will cost you two, as will "driving too fast for conditions" at speeds of 10 mph or less. Speeding 11–25 mph over the limit is worth four points, as is any instance above 10 mph considered too fast for conditions. Reckless riding and speeding at 25 mph or more above the limit are both worth six. Two reckless convictions within five years will get you suspended for three months. Racing will get you revoked. Habitual offenders are defined as having committed three or more major offenses (pretty bad ones) or any combination of 10 minor offenses (four or more points each) within three years. Habitual offenders get a five-year suspension.

HELMET LAW: Riders and passengers younger than 21 are required to wear helmets. Reflectorization is also required, with a minimum of four square inches of reflectorized material on both sides of the helmet if the helmet itself is not reflectorized.

EYE PROTECTION: Glasses, goggles, a face shield, or a suitable windshield is required for riders under 21.

PERMIT RESTRICTIONS: A rider operating under a permit cannot ride between 6 p.m. (8 p.m. during daylight savings!) and 6 a.m. unless accompanied by a motorcycle-endorsed parent or guardian. At other times of day, you must be accompanied by an adult driver (21 or older) with a motorcycle license and at least one year of riding experience.

UNCHANGING TRAFFIC SIGNAL LAW: After waiting for two minutes, the motorcyclist may proceed carefully through an unchanging red light, treating it as if it were a stop sign.

LICENSE PLATE DISPLAY: No letter or number on the plate can be obstructed by a frame or a clear or tinted shield.

EQUIPMENT REQUIREMENTS: Bikes are required to have at least one rearview mirror and a passenger seat and footrests if carrying a passenger.

GOOD RESOURCES

South Carolina Department of Motor Vehicles: www.scdmvonline.com
South Carolina Vehicle Code: www.scstatehouse.gov/code/titl56.htm

42

SOUTH DAKOTA

RIDEABILITY RANK: 10

With a higher ranking being best for motorcyclists, South Dakota ranks fifth in the nation for population density and 14th for law enforcement density. South Dakota is a farming and ranching grasslands state boasting low mountains and the thick forests of the Black Hills. Roadways tend to be straight and wide, except for the Black Hills Area, where they're scenic, winding, and hilly. The ratio of multi-vehicle motorcycle fatalities to single-vehicle motorcycle fatalities is 55/45. The typical patrol vehicle is a Ford Police Interceptor (Crown Vic) with an occasional Tahoe or Durango. The overall tone of law enforcement toward motorcycle riders is best described as businesslike.

SOUTH DAKOTA AT A GLANCE

Helmet Law	Partial	Exhaust Noise	No
Eye Protection	Required by law	Earphones	Okay
Permit Restrictions	Yes	Checkpoints	Yes
Insurance	25/50/25	Automated Enforcement	Red light cameras
Reciprocity	Yes	School Buses	Yes
Handlebar Height Restriction	Yes	Pedestrians	Yes
Daytime Headlight Use	Not required	Move-Over Law	Yes
Left Lane Restriction	No	Excessive Speed Sanctions	No
Unchanging Traffic Signal Law	None	Mandatory Tow	No
Turn Signals	Not required	Feet Down	No
License Plate Display	Yes	Erratics	Yes
Fenders	Not required		

For more detailed information on the above, see next page or reference Chapter 2: U.S. Motorcycle Laws and Regulations.

SOUTH DAKOTA LAWS IN DETAIL

South Dakota uses a demerit points system, and a very spare one at that, to track moving violations. Drivers who accrue 15 points in a year or 22 points in two years may be suspended. Reckless driving costs you eight points; eluding or racing costs you six; failure to yield, improper passing, or driving on the wrong side of the road is worth four; most others are worth two. Speeding tickets are not accompanied by any demerit points at all.

HELMET LAW: Riders and passengers younger than 18 are required to wear helmets that meets FMVSS 218 standards.

EYE PROTECTION: Operators must wear glasses, goggles, or a face shield unless the motorcycle is equipped with a windscreen.

PERMIT RESTRICTIONS: A rider on a permit may ride only between 6 a.m. and 8 p.m. and only if accompanied by a licensed rider 18 or older who has at least one year of riding experience and is riding a separate motorcycle. Permitted riders may not carry passengers.

HANDLEBAR HEIGHT RESTRICTION: Handgrips must fall below shoulder height while the operator is seated on the motorcycle.

LICENSE PLATE DISPLAY: Plates are required to be conspicuously displayed, securely fastened, horizontal and upright, and kept clean and clearly visible.

EQUIPMENT REQUIREMENTS: Motorcycles are required to have at least one rearview mirror as well as a passenger seat and footrests if carrying a passenger.

ERRATICS: Glazing on motorcycle windscreens must be clear. No demerit points are given for speeding.

GOOD RESOURCES

South Dakota Department of Public Safety: http://dps.sd.gov
South Dakota Codified Laws: http://legis.state.sd.us

TENNESSEE

RIDEABILITY RANK: 40

With a higher ranking being best for motorcyclists, Tennessee ranks 31st in the nation for population density and 38th for law enforcement density. Tennessee is a lush, diverse state with spectacular mountains, rolling hills, and fertile valleys. Roadways tend to be well maintained and almost 100 percent paved. The ratio of multi-vehicle motorcycle fatalities to single-vehicle motorcycle fatalities is 57/43. The typical patrol vehicle is a Ford Police Interceptor (Crown Vic) or Chevy Impala. The overall tone of law enforcement toward motorcycle riders is best described as businesslike.

TENNESSEE LAWS IN DETAIL

Tennessee uses a demerit points system to track moving violations. An adult 18 or older with 12 points in a year will be suspended. A minor with six points in a year will be suspended. Two reckless ridings within a year, racing, or being a habitual violator

TENNESSEE AT A GLANCE

Helmet Law	Yes		Earphones	Okay
Eye Protection	Required by law		Checkpoints	Yes
Permit Restrictions	No		Automated Enforcement	Speed, red light cameras
Insurance	25/50/10			
Reciprocity	No		School Buses	Yes
Handlebar Height Restriction	None		Pedestrians	Yes
Daytime Headlight Use	Required by law		Move-Over Law	Yes
Left Lane Restriction	Yes		Excessive Speed Sanctions	No
Unchanging Traffic Signal Law	Yes		Mandatory Tow	No
Turn Signals	Not required		HOV	Okay
License Plate Display	Yes		Feet Down	No
Fenders	Not required		Erratics	Yes
Exhaust Noise	No			

For more detailed information on the above, see next page or reference Chapter 2: U.S. Motorcycle Laws and Regulations.

can all get you suspended or revoked. Exceeding the speed limit by even 1 mph in a school zone can be considered reckless driving. Once every five years, you can complete a driver improvement clinic to avoid or shorten a suspension.

Speeding 1–5 mph over the limit is worth one point. Getting nicked for 6–15 mph over is worth three; 16–25 is worth four; 26–35 is worth five; 36–45 is worth six; and 46 or more above the limit is worth eight points. Point totals go up significantly if you're speeding in a construction zone. Contributing to a crash is worth three or four points. Reckless is worth six, and a school bus violation is worth eight.

HELMET LAW: All riders and passengers must wear helmets that compliy with FMVSS 218 standards. However, riders 21 and older may wear helmets that do not meet the FMVSS 218 penetration, continuous contour, and labeling standards. These helmets must have labels noting compliance with ASTM, CSPM, or Snell standards. A rider 18 and older can go without the helmet when riding in a parade at less than 30 mph.

EYE PROTECTION: Glasses, goggles, or a face shield is required unless the motorcycle is equipped with a windscreen.

PERMIT RESTRICTIONS: There are plenty of permit restrictions in Tennessee, but they apply only to Tennessee riders who are 15 and hold a motorcycle learner's permit.

RECIPROCITY: Tennessee is not a member of the mostly nationwide Driver License Compact. The purpose of the compact is to assist states in administering the "one license, one driving record" concept. The only states remaining that don't adhere to the concept are Georgia, Massachusetts, Michigan, Tennessee, and Wisconsin. This doesn't mean that your home state won't find out about the ticket you received in one of these states, but it does mean you have a better chance of slipping by if you do.

LEFT LANE RESTRICTION: It is illegal to travel in the left lane of an interstate slower than 55 mph (under normal weather conditions) unless congestion makes it impossible to go faster.

UNCHANGING TRAFFIC SIGNAL LAW: If a motorcyclist is stuck at an unchanging red light, and the device is the type that detects the presence of motor vehicles, the rider may proceed using due care and caution after coming to a complete stop. However, you'll be stuck with a ticket if it's a timed light that you "believed" was a sensor-operated signal, so make absolutely sure it's a sensor signal before blowing the red.

LICENSE PLATE DISPLAY: Plates must be securely fastened in a horizontal position to prevent swinging and be at a height of no less than 12 inches. They must also be clearly visible, with no tinted materials. Motorcycles with vertically mounted plate brackets are okay if the top of the plate is fastened along the right vertical edge (meaning you'd have to tilt your head to the right to read the plate).

EQUIPMENT REQUIREMENTS: Motorcycles must have at least one rearview mirror, a passenger seat and footrests if carrying a passenger, and a working speedometer.

ERRATICS: Taillight modulators that flash for five seconds before showing a continuous light are specifically legal in Tennessee.

GOOD RESOURCE

Tennessee Laws and Policies; Department of Safety and Homeland Security: www.tn.gov

TEXAS

RIDEABILITY RANK: 33

With a higher ranking being best for motorcyclists, Texas ranks 24th in the nation for population density and 32nd for law enforcement density. Texas is an expansive state with seashore, forests, plains, desert, and mountains. Roadways tend to be well maintained regardless of terrain and ripe with deer. The ratio of multi-vehicle motorcycle fatalities to single-vehicle motorcycle fatalities is 56/44. Texas is known informally as a state notorious for writing traffic tickets. There is no typical patrol vehicle in Texas, but watch for Ford Police Interceptors (Crown Vics), of which there are *thousands*. Texas law enforcement uses family sedans, SUVs, hot rods, and pickups. Motorcycle officers ride a variety of makes. The overall tone of law enforcement toward motorcycle riders is best described as businesslike with aggressive exceptions.

TEXAS AT A GLANCE

Helmet Law	Partial	Exhaust Noise	No
Eye Protection	Not required	Earphones	Okay
Permit Restrictions	Yes	Checkpoints	No
Insurance	20/50/25	Automated Enforcement	Red light cameras
Reciprocity	Yes	School Buses	Yes
Handlebar Height Restriction	Yes	Pedestrians	Yes
Daytime Headlight Use	Required by law	Move-Over Law	Yes
Left Lane Restriction	None	Excessive Speed Sanctions	No
Unchanging Traffic Signal Law	No	Mandatory Tow	No
Turn Signals	Not required	Feet Down	No
License Plate Display	Yes	Erratics	Yes
Fenders	Not required		

For more detailed information on the above, see next page or reference Chapter 2: U.S. Motorcycle Laws and Regulations.

TEXAS LAWS IN DETAIL

Collecting four moving violations in a year or seven in two years will get your license suspended. Not fun.

But wait, there's more. Texas uses a unique points system to track moving violation convictions. Drivers who rack up large numbers of points pay additional administrative fees annually just for the privilege of being a problem driver. Moving violations are worth two points; a moving violation resulting in a crash is worth three. These points apply to convictions within or outside of Texas, and the fees go above and beyond the usual fine for a citation, administrative fees, surcharges, etc.

Six points within three years is where the trouble starts. At that point, the driver will be required to pay $100 a year for those six points—plus an additional $25 per point above six—every year until the point total drops below six. Doing something *really* dumb (DWI, no insurance, etc.) means you'll pay these fees for three straight years: $1,000 a year for your first DWI, for example, or $250 a year for an invalid license or no insurance. Don't even ask what happens if you're a repeat offender or blow a 0.16 or more on a breathalyzer. In a word (or four): Don't mess with Texas.

HELMET LAW: Riders under 21 are required to wear helmets that meet FMVSS 218 standards. Riders 21 and older who have completed a rider education course or can show proof that they have health insurance are exempt from the helmet requirement. These exemptions should be considered "secondary" offenses, meaning that law enforcement does not pull you over because you're not wearing your helmet just to check compliance.

PERMIT RESTRICTIONS: A rider on a permit ("learner license") is permitted to ride only within sight of a licensed motorcyclist 21 or older.

HANDLEBAR HEIGHT RESTRICTION: Handlebar height is restricted to no more than 15 inches above the lowest part of the operator's seat.

DAYTIME HEADLIGHT USE: Use of the motorcycle's headlight during daylight hours is mandatory if your bike is 1975 or newer.

LICENSE PLATE DISPLAY: Plates cannot have any covers or stickers that affect the plate's color, detectability, or readability or obstruct any letters, numbers, or official tags.

EQUIPMENT REQUIREMENTS: Motorcycles are required to have at least one rearview mirror, a passenger seat if carrying a passenger, and an annual inspection.

ERRATICS: If you ride without a helmet, you're required to either have completed a motorcycle rider education course or be able to show proof that you have medical insurance. If your vehicle is leaking fluids that could be considered a hazard or threat, it can be towed away for that reason alone. Be aware that more than a few Texas police officers don't consider a motorcycle fully stopped at a stop sign until one foot has touched the ground. Of course, there's nothing in the Texas statutes that confirms this, but beware all the same.

GOOD RESOURCES

Texas Department of Public Safety: www.txdps.state.tx.us
Texas Transportation Code: www.statutes.legis.state.tx.us

UTAH

RIDEABILITY RANK: 14

With a higher ranking being best for motorcyclists, Utah ranks tenth in the nation for population density and 8th for law enforcement density. Utah is a scenic, mountainous state with red rocks, twisty roads, and canyon deserts. Roadways tend to be wide, hilly, and twisty. The ratio of multi-vehicle motorcycle fatalities to single-vehicle motorcycle fatalities is 57/43. The typical patrol vehicle is a Ford Police Interceptor (Crown Vic) or Dodge Charger. The overall tone of law enforcement toward motorcycle riders is best described as businesslike.

UTAH LAWS IN DETAIL
You can lose your license if you are over 70 points and under 21 years of age. Those over 21 can lose their license if they have accumulated 200 points during a three-year period. Utah's handbook is online; part is Utah laws and part is MSF. Some is in Utah Code Annotated 53-3-901.

UTAH AT A GLANCE

Helmet Law	Partial	Exhaust Noise	Yes
Eye Protection	No	Earphones	Okay
Permit Restrictions	Yes	Checkpoints	Yes
Insurance	25/50/15, No-fault	Automated Enforcement	No
		School Buses	Yes
Reciprocity	Yes	Pedestrians	Yes
Handlebar Height Restriction	Yes	Move-Over Law	Yes
Daytime Headlight Use	Not required	Excessive Speed Sanctions	No
Left Lane Restriction	Yes	Mandatory Tow	No
Unchanging Traffic Signal Law	None	HOV:	Okay
Turn Signals	Required by law	Feet Down	No
License Plate Display	Yes	Erratics	Yes
Fenders	Required by law		

For more detailed information on the above, see next page or reference Chapter 2: U.S. Motorcycle Laws and Regulations.

Utah uses a demerit points system to track license violations. If you're 21 or older, collecting 200 points within a three-year period gets you a required administrative hearing. If you're younger than 21, this process begins at 70 points. At this hearing, you may get suspended or sent to a driver improvement clinic—or both. Reckless riding will cost you 80 points; speeding citations run 35, 55, and 75 points depending on the scope of the violation. Suspensions can be three, six, or 12 months depending on your driving record. Convictions remain on your driving record for three years.

Two reckless convictions in a year will get you revoked. Committing two or more traffic infractions at a time, or during the same "driving event," brings your citation up to "careless."

Keeping your driving record sparkly clean removes points from your record. If you are conviction-free for one year, your points are reduced by half. Being conviction-free for two years in a row removes all points from your record. You can also deduct 50 points every three years by enrolling in a driver improvement clinic.

HELMET LAW: All riders younger than 18 are required to wear helmets that meet FMVSS 218 requirements. It is interesting to note that if you're 18 or older and were wearing a helmet at the time of your citation, your fine will be reduced by $8.

PERMIT RESTRICTIONS: For the first two months of the permit, riders may not carry passengers or ride on roadways with a posted limit of 60 mph or more, and they may not ride between the hours of 10 p.m. and 6 a.m.

HANDLEBAR HEIGHT RESTRICTION: Handlebars may rise to a level no higher than the operator's shoulders while he or she is seated on the bike.

LEFT LANE RESTRICTION: Drivers in the left lane on a multi-lane freeway must yield to vehicles approaching from behind and cannot impede the flow of traffic.

TURN SIGNALS: All motorcycles manufactured after January 1, 1973, must have turn signals if originally equipped with them. Operators must signal intent to turn or change lanes at least two full seconds in advance.

LICENSE PLATE DISPLAY: License plates must be displayed horizontally to be read from left to right. They must be visible from 100 feet, securely mounted, and clearly visible.

FENDERS: Fenders cannot be missing, improperly mounted, cracked, or bent or have sharp edges. The front fender must cover the wheel to at least 45 degrees on the front and 45 degrees on the rear. The rear fender must cover the top half of the tire.

EXHAUST NOISE: Exhausts must be properly mounted, secure, and functioning. The pipe cannot be altered to be anything less effective than the original equipment.

EQUIPMENT REQUIREMENTS: A left-side rearview mirror is required, as is a passenger seat and footrests if carrying a passenger. A working odometer, fenders front and rear, and an annual inspection are required.

ERRATICS: If you get a speeding citation on a freeway and the speed is 10 mph or less, then the citation won't go on your driving record.

GOOD RESOURCES

Utah Department of Public Safety: http://publicsafety.utah.gov
Utah Administrative Rules: www.rules.utah.gov
Utah Statutes and Code 53-3-901: http://le.utah.gov

VERMONT

RIDEABILITY RANK: 19

With a higher ranking being best for motorcyclists, Vermont ranks 20th in the nation for population density and seventh for law enforcement density. Vermont is a scenic mountain state with an inordinate number of deer and moose. Roadways tend to be winding and narrow. The ratio of multi-vehicle motorcycle fatalities to single-vehicle motorcycle fatalities is 63/37. The typical patrol vehicle is a Ford Police Interceptor (Crown Vic). The overall tone of law enforcement toward motorcycle riders is best described as businesslike.

VERMONT LAWS IN DETAIL

Vermont uses a points system for moving violations. Points are assigned after a conviction. Speeding will get you two to eight points depending on your speed. Excessive speed, defined as 20 mph or more over the limit, can get you six points depending on where it happens. Texting will get you two to five points. Failing to stop for a stop sign or signal is two points, and failing to obey law enforcement is four

VERMONT AT A GLANCE

Helmet Law	Yes	Exhaust Noise	Yes
Eye Protection	Required by law	Earphones	Okay
Permit Restrictions	Yes	Checkpoints	Yes
Insurance	25/50/10	Automated Enforcement	No
Reciprocity	Normally No	School Buses	Yes
Handlebar Height Restriction	Yes	Pedestrians	Yes
Daytime Headlight Use	Not required	Move-Over Law	Yes
Left Lane Restriction	Yes	Excessive Speed Sanctions	No
Unchanging Traffic Signal Law	No	Mandatory Tow	No
Turn Signals	Required by law	Feet Down	No
License Plate Display	Yes	Erratics	Yes
Fenders	Required by law		

For more detailed information on the above, see next page or reference Chapter 2: U.S. Motorcycle Laws and Regulations.

points. Failure to yield to an emergency vehicle or law enforcement is five points, failure to yield to pedestrian in a crosswalk is four points, and failure to stop for a school bus is five points.

Once you hit 10 points, you'll get a letter telling you that your license will be suspended. The number of points you've accumulated within two years will determine how long you'll be suspended. The more points, the longer the suspension. Points are not given for parking or equipment violations.

HELMET LAW: FMVSS 218–compliant helmets are required for all riders and passengers. Reflectorization of the helmet is required.

EYE PROTECTION: Glasses, goggles, or a face shield is required unless the bike has a windshield. Operators are prohibited from wearing tinted lenses at night.

PERMIT RESTRICTIONS: Vermont only recognizes motorcycle permits issued by the Vermont DMV. In other words, if you have a motorcycle permit from another state, you cannot ride in Vermont. Riders on Vermont permits are restricted to daytime operation only. They cannot carry passengers, and it is implied that riding is limited to Vermont only. The state suggests that you contact other states in which you plan to ride to ask if they honor Vermont motorcycle permits.

RECIPROCITY: Normally no. However, if an individual's right to operate a motor vehicle in Vermont is suspended, his or her home state is notified.

HANDLEBAR HEIGHT RESTRICTION: Handlebar height shall not be more than 15 inches above the operator's seat.

LEFT LANE RESTRICTION: Unless there are signs stating otherwise, drivers shall keep to the right except to pass.

TURN SIGNALS: You are required to have turn signals if the motorcycle was originally equipped with turn signals.

LICENSE PLATE DISPLAY: Plates must be securely mounted, clearly visible, mounted in a position where it will be illuminated by plate light, and mounted horizontally.

EXHAUST NOISE: The exhaust system shall be deemed defective if any changes, modifications, alterations, deletions, or adjustments have been made that would thereby cause any exhaust system to generate a higher sound level than would be generated by the exhaust system customarily installed by the manufacturer as original equipment.

EQUIPMENT REQUIREMENTS: At least one mirror is required, as are front and rear fenders. A passenger seat, footrests, and handholds are required if you carry a passenger. An inspection is required.

ERRATICS: Inspection is required once a year. Inspectors look over your bike and equipment very, very carefully.

Vermont is one of only two states in the nation in which riding side-by-side (two abreast) is illegal. However, the penalty for violating this law is only minor. The other state is Virginia, in which the penalty is potentially much more severe.

GOOD RESOURCES
Vermont Division of Motor Vehicles: www.dmv.vermont.gov
Vermont State Statutes Title 23: www.leg.state.vt.us

47

VIRGINIA

RIDEABILITY RANK: 36

With a higher ranking being best for motorcyclists, Virginia ranks 36th in the nation for population density and 45th for law enforcement density. Virginia is a mountain state with coastal plains, heavy forests, and rivers. The ratio of multi-vehicle motorcycle fatalities to single-vehicle motorcycle fatalities is 45/55. Virginia is known informally as a state notorious for writing traffic tickets. The typical patrol vehicle runs the gamut from Ford Police Interceptors (Crown Vics) and Chargers to Chevy Impalas and Dodge Intrepids. The overall tone of law enforcement toward motorcycle riders is best described as businesslike.

VIRGINIA LAWS IN DETAIL

Virginia uses a demerit points system to track moving violations. If you're 18 or older, getting 12 points in 12 months or 18 points in 24 months will get you enrolled in a driver improvement clinic. Any demerit points violation you received at age 18 or 19 will require an even more stringent driver improvement clinic. Getting nicked for 18 points in a year or 24 points in two years will get you suspended for 90 days and require completion of a driver improvement clinic.

VIRGINIA AT A GLANCE

Helmet Law	Yes	Exhaust Noise	Yes
Eye Protection	Required by law	Earphones	One ear only
Permit Restrictions	Yes	Checkpoints	Yes
Insurance	25/50/20	Automated Enforcement	Red light cameras
Reciprocity	Yes	School Buses	Yes
Handlebar Height Restriction	None	Pedestrians	Yes
Daytime Headlight Use	Not required	Move-Over Law	Yes
Left Lane Restriction	None	Excessive Speed Sanctions	Yes
Unchanging Traffic Signal Law	Yes	Mandatory Tow	No
Turn Signals	Not required	HOV	Okay
License Plate Display	Yes	Feet Down	No
Fenders	Not required	Erratics	Yes

For more detailed information on the above, see next page or reference Chapter 2: U.S. Motorcycle Laws and Regulations.

Points remain on your record for two years from the date you commit the offense, not the conviction. Speeding at less than 10 mph over the limit will cost you three points, as will many other minor violations. Traveling at 10–19 mph above the limit will cost you four. Speeding 20 mph or more above the limit, or traveling at 81 mph or greater (considered reckless), will cost you six points.

Lots of things in Virginia can be considered reckless driving: racing, school bus violations, failing to signal properly, and even obstructed view.

You will receive five safe driving points if you voluntarily complete a driver improvement clinic.

HELMET LAW: Operators and passengers are required to wear helmets that conform to DOT, ANSI, or Snell standards.

EYE PROTECTION: Glasses, goggles, or a face shield is required unless the motorcycle is equipped with an approved windscreen.

PERMIT RESTRICTIONS: A rider on a permit may ride only between 4 a.m. and midnight. You must be supervised by a motorcycle-endorsed adult 21 or older and may not carry passengers. A parent, guardian, or sibling can supervise you if he or she is licensed as a motorcyclist and 18 or older.

UNCHANGING TRAFFIC SIGNAL LAW: Virginia provides accommodations for motorcycle, moped, and bicycle riders stuck at a red light that does not recognize your vehicle. Once the rider has come to a complete stop and then waited through two light cycles or two minutes, he or she may proceed through the red light when it is safe to do so but must yield to any traffic that has the green light (right of way).

LICENSE PLATE DISPLAY: Plates must be securely fastened and clearly visible, including all letters, numbers, or decals.

EXHAUST NOISE: Exhaust systems cannot produce more noise than the bike did when stock, and it is illegal to run a bike with a gutted muffler or a straight pipe.

EARPHONES: Headphones or earphones are permitted in one ear only. Speakers mounted inside a helmet are okay.

EXCESSIVE SPEED SANCTIONS: Hooboy. In Virginia, reckless driving is treated as a criminal offense and can get you up to a $2,500 ticket, a year in jail, or a six-month suspension. It is critical to note that 20 mph over the limit or 81 mph or above anywhere is considered reckless.

EQUIPMENT REQUIREMENTS: At least one rearview mirror is required, as are a passenger seat and footrests if you carry a passenger. Motorcycles are inspected annually.

ERRATICS: Even failure to signal a turn can be considered reckless driving. Radar detectors are illegal in Virginia. And get this: Virginia is one of only two states in the nation in which riding side-by-side with another motorcycle (known in the other 48 states as riding "two abreast") is illegal. This violation is classified as a misdemeanor, which can carry up to a $2,500 fine and 12 months in jail. The other state that does not allow motorcycles riding two abreast is Vermont.

GOOD RESOURCES
Virginia Department of Motor Vehicles: http://www.dmv.state.va.us
Virginia Motor Vehicle Code 46.2: http://leg1.state.va.us

48

WASHINGTON

RIDEABILITY RANK: 12

With a higher ranking being best for motorcyclists, Washington ranks 25th in the nation for population density and first for law enforcement density. Washington is a scenic mountain, river-valley, lakes, high-desert, and coastal state. Roadways tend to be of all sorts, from busy interstates and multi-lane highways to narrow, winding country roads. The ratio of multi-vehicle motorcycle fatalities to single-vehicle motorcycle fatalities is 54/46. Patrol vehicles in Washington come in all shapes and sizes, marked and unmarked, but the state relies heavily on the Ford Police Interceptors (Crown Vics) and various SUVs. The overall tone of law enforcement toward motorcycle riders is best described as businesslike. However, Washington law enforcement controls speeding tightly. The informal expectation is if you're more than 5 mph over, you'll get stopped.

WASHINGTON AT A GLANCE

Helmet Law	Yes	Exhaust Noise	Yes
Eye Protection	Required by law	Earphones	Prohibited by law
Permit Restrictions	Yes	Checkpoints	No
Insurance	Not required for motorcycles (25/50/10 for other vehicles)	Automated Enforcement	Speed, red light cameras, rail crossings
		School Buses	Yes
Reciprocity	Yes	Pedestrians	Yes
Handlebar Height Restriction	Yes	Move-Over Law	Yes
Daytime Headlight Use	Required by law	Excessive Speed Sanctions	Yes
Left Lane Restriction	Yes	Mandatory Tow	No
Unchanging Traffic Signal Law	No	HOV	Okay
Turn Signals	Required by law	Feet Down	No
License Plate Display	Yes	Erratics	Yes
Fenders	Required by law		

For more detailed information on the above, see next page or reference Chapter 2: U.S. Motorcycle Laws and Regulations.

WASHINGTON LAWS IN DETAIL

Washington does not use a demerit points system. Instead, frequent flyers have their licenses suspended or they are put on probation. You earn a 60-day suspension for six moving violations within 12 months. You'll be put in a conditional status or on probation if you get nicked for four moving violations in a 12-month period, or five within 24 months.

If you're on probation and you rack up two more violations, you get a 30-day suspension and another year of probation. During this extended probation, one moving violation will get you suspended again. The duration of these suspensions gets longer the more you earn: The first is 30 days, second is 60, third is 120, fourth and beyond is 364.

HELMET LAW: A helmet meeting the requirements of FMVSS 218 is required for all riders.

EYE PROTECTION: Glasses, goggles or a face shield is required by law unless your bike is equipped with a windscreen.

PERMIT RESTRICTIONS: A rider on a permit can operate during daylight hours only and may not carry passengers.

INSURANCE: Yep, believe it or not, motorcycle riders are not required to carry liability insurance in the state of Washington. Nor are motor-driven cycle or moped riders required to have insurance. Proceed with caution—remember, liability insurance protects you.

HANDLEBAR HEIGHT RESTRICTION: Handlebars can rise no more than 30 inches above the operator's seat.

TURN SIGNALS: Electric turn signals are required by law for any motorcycle built later than 1952.

LICENSE PLATE DISPLAY: License plates must be illuminated and mounted in a horizontal position.

FENDERS: Front and rear fenders, as wide as the tire, are required by law.

EXHAUST NOISE: It is illegal to modify an exhaust system in a manner that increases the noise emitted above the stock level.

EARPHONES: While earphones are not legal, helmets with built-in speakers are okay.

EXCESSIVE SPEED SANCTIONS: When combined with any other violation, a minor speeding violation can quickly turn into a reckless driving citation, which can carry jail time of up to a year and a $5,000 fine. Washington also uses a catchall law (Negligent Driving Second Degree), which ascribes negligence and endangerment to person or property and can lead to an immediate arrest in instances such as hot-rodding, showboating, or one-wheeling.

EQUIPMENT REQUIREMENTS: Motorcycles are required to have rearview mirrors left and right, fenders front and rear, and a passenger seat and footrests if you're carrying a passenger. Turn signals are required, and expect to submit to random inspections.

ERRATICS: Liability insurance is not required for motorcycles in the state of Washington.

GOOD RESOURCES

Washington State Statutes: http://apps.leg.wa.gov/RCW/default.aspx?cite=46
Department of Licensing: www.dol.wa.gov

WEST VIRGINIA

RIDEABILITY RANK: 6

With a higher ranking being best for motorcyclists, West Virginia ranks 21st in the nation for population density and fourth for law enforcement density. West Virginia is a rugged, mountainous mining state with dense forests. The ratio of multi-vehicle motorcycle fatalities to single-vehicle motorcycle fatalities is 43/57. The typical patrol vehicle is a Ford Police Interceptor (Crown Vic) or Dodge Durango. The overall tone of law enforcement toward motorcycle riders is best described as businesslike.

WEST VIRGINIA AT A GLANCE

Helmet Law	Yes	Exhaust Noise	No
Eye Protection	Required by law	Earphones	Okay
Permit Restrictions	Yes	Checkpoints	Yes
Insurance	20/40/10	Automated Enforcement	No
Reciprocity	Yes	School Buses	Yes
Handlebar Height Restriction	Yes	Pedestrians	Yes
Daytime Headlight Use	Required by law	Move-Over Law	Yes
Left Lane Restriction	None	Excessive Speed Sanctions	No
Unchanging Traffic Signal Law	None	Mandatory Tow	No
Turn Signals	Not required	Feet Down	No
License Plate Display	No	Erratics	None
Fenders	Not required		

For more detailed information on the above, see next page or reference Chapter 2: U.S. Motorcycle Laws and Regulations.

WEST VIRGINIA LAWS IN DETAIL

West Virginia uses a points system to track moving violations. Points remain on your record for two years after conviction; the infraction itself remains for five years. When you reach 12 points, expect to have your license suspended for 30 days. At 14 points, it's 45 days; at 16 points, 60 days; at 18 points, 90 days; and at 20 or more points, your license is suspended until you're down to 11 points again as they drop off your record two years later. Three reckless convictions in 24 months, or racing, will get you immediately revoked.

Speeding tickets below 5 mph over the limit do not carry points. At 5-9 mph over, the penalty is two points. Traveling at 10-14 over is worth three points, while 15 or greater is worth five. Reckless and speeding in a school zone (any speed) is worth six—equivalent to a hit-and-run. Drivers can have three points dropped from their record once every two years by completing an approved driver improvement clinic. These defensive driving courses can sometimes be used to stave off a suspension.

HELMET LAW: All riders and passengers are required to wear helmets that conform to DOT, ANSI, or Snell standards.

EYE PROTECTION: Glasses, goggles, or a face shield is required by law.

PERMIT RESTRICTIONS: A rider on a permit can only ride during daylight hours and may not carry passengers.

HANDLEBAR HEIGHT RESTRICTION: Handgrips can rise to no more than 15 inches above the operator's seat.

EQUIPMENT REQUIREMENTS: Every bike is required to have at least one rearview mirror, a passenger seat and footrests if carrying a passenger, and an annual inspection.

GOOD RESOURCES

West Virginia Division of Motor Vehicles: www.transportation.wv.gov
West Virginia Vehicle Code Chapter 17: www.legis.state.wv.us

WISCONSIN

RIDEABILITY RANK: 18

With a higher ranking being best for motorcyclists, Wisconsin ranks 27th in the nation for population density and 26th for law enforcement density. Wisconsin has scenic lake areas, breathtaking river valleys, and hilly farmlands—and a lot of deer. Roadways tend to be well paved with predictable curves, though river valleys and coulees hold some twisting, challenging routes. The ratio of multi-vehicle motorcycle fatalities to single-vehicle motorcycle fatalities is 47/53. The typical patrol vehicle is a Ford Police Interceptor (Crown Vic). The overall tone of law enforcement toward motorcycle riders is best described as businesslike.

WISCONSIN AT A GLANCE

Helmet Law	**Partial**	Exhaust Noise	**Yes**
Eye Protection	**Required by law**	Earphones	**Okay**
Permit Restrictions	**Yes**	Checkpoints	**No**
Insurance	**25/50/10**	Automated Enforcement	**No**
Reciprocity	**No**	School Buses	**Yes**
Handlebar Height Restriction	**Yes**	Pedestrians	**Yes**
Daytime Headlight Use	**Required by law**	Move-Over Law	**Yes**
Left Lane Restriction	**None**	Excessive Speed Sanctions	**No**
Unchanging Traffic Signal Law	**Yes**	Mandatory Tow	**No**
Turn Signals	**Not required**	HOV	**Okay**
License Plate Display	**Yes**	Feet Down	**No**
Fenders	**Required by law**	Erratics	**None**

For more detailed information on the above, see next page or reference Chapter 2: U.S. Motorcycle Laws and Regulations.

WISCONSIN LAWS IN DETAIL

Wisconsin uses a demerit points system to track moving violations. Points are assessed as of the date of the violation, not the conviction. You could have your license suspended for a ticket that you ultimately fight and win, so watch yourself. If you hold a probationary license, points double. If you rack up 12 points in a year, a mandatory suspension of two months will ensue.

Speeding 20 mph or more is worth six points, equivalent to reckless riding or a DUI. (That says more about Wisconsin's attitude toward DWI than it says about its attitude toward speeding.) In a 55- to 65-mph zone, you can also be looking at an instant 15-day suspension for traveling 25 mph or more over the limit. Speeding 11–19 mph over the limit will cost you four points. Getting nicked for 1–10 mph over is worth two.

Most other violations are worth two to four points. Forgoing eye protection on a motorcycle will cost you two points. A handlebar ticket will also cost you two. Once every three years, you can complete an approved driver improvement clinic (including a motorcycle safety course) to have three points removed from your record.

Wisconsin identifies habitual violators as those who have 12 or more moving violation convictions (speeding, etc.), four or more major violations within five years, or a combination of major and minor convictions numbering 12.

Wisconsin is not a member of the Nonresident Violator Compact (NRVC), which is meant to ensure equal treatment of nonresidents and residents and standardize methods for processing citations, as well as the response of the rider/driver to comply to them. This means that if you're nabbed for a moving violation here, the arresting officer is not obligated to release you without posting bond for the fine. If you don't have a method of posting bond (cash works; checks and credit may work), you could end up in jail until you do. If you are required to pay the fine or appear in court and fail to do so, your home state will not necessarily suspend your license until you comply with the citation's requirements (pay the fine)—they may never even know about it. States that are not members of this compact are Alaska, California, Michigan, Montana, Oregon, and Wisconsin.

HELMET LAW: A helmet that meets FMVSS 218 requirements is required for riders and passengers younger than 18 and those riding on a permit.

EYE PROTECTION: Glasses, goggles, or a face shield is required unless the motorcycle is equipped with an approved windshield. An approved windshield must rise at least 15 inches above the handlebars to qualify. Tinted or darkened eye protection at night is illegal.

PERMIT RESTRICTIONS: An FMVSS-compliant motorcycle helmet is required for a rider on a permit. Passengers can only be licensed motorcyclists with at least two years experience. Permitted riders cannot ride at night unless they're accompanied (as a passenger or on/in another vehicle) by a licensed motorcyclist with at least two years driving experience.

RECIPROCITY: Wisconsin is not a member of the mostly nationwide Driver License Compact. The purpose of the compact is to assist states in administering the "one license, one driving record" concept. The only states remaining that don't adhere to the concept are Georgia, Massachusetts, Michigan, Tennessee, and Wisconsin. This doesn't mean that your home state won't find out about the ticket you received in one of these states, but it does mean you have a better chance of slipping by.

HANDLEBAR HEIGHT RESTRICTION: Handgrips can rise to no more than 30 inches above the operator's seat.

UNCHANGING TRAFFIC SIGNAL LAW: Wisconsin offers an escape route for riders faced with an unchanging red light. If you "reasonably believe" the light activates on a signal and it has not recognized your bike, you can proceed through the red light if no other vehicles are present to activate the signal, you have stopped for at least 45 seconds, and you yield right-of-way to any vehicles proceeding through a green light as well as to any pedestrians and bicycles there. If you don't adhere to all these conditions, it can be considered a failure to yield right-of-way ticket . . . which also requires a trip to traffic school.

LICENSE PLATE DISPLAY: Plates must be attached firmly and rigidly in a horizontal position and conspicuous place. Plates have to be legible (free of dirt and foreign substances) so they can be easily seen and read. Failure to comply comes with a fine up to $200.

EXHAUST NOISE: Exhausts cannot be modified to be louder than the OEM equipment—although anyone who's ever spent time in the great state of Wisconsin knows that this rule is seldom enforced.

EQUIPMENT REQUIREMENTS: Motorcycles are required to have at least one rearview mirror, a rear fender, a passenger seat and footrests if carrying a passenger, and a working speedometer and odometer. They may be subjected to random inspections. Never a good time.

GOOD RESOURCE

Wisconsin Department of Transportation and Motor Vehicle Laws:
www.dot.wisconsin.gov

WYOMING

RIDEABILITY RANK: 15

With a higher ranking being best for motorcyclists, Wyoming ranks second in the nation for population density and 47th for law enforcement density. Wyoming is a prairie, mountain, and river state. Prairie roadways tend to be flat, straight, and windy (gusts). Mountain roadways tend to be winding and scenic. Animals such as deer, antelope, and buffalo roam Wyoming freely, so avoid riding at night, dusk, and dawn. The ratio of multi-vehicle motorcycle fatalities to single-vehicle motorcycle fatalities is 40/60. The typical patrol vehicle is a Ford Crown Vic or Dodge Charger. The overall tone of law enforcement toward motorcycle riders is best described as businesslike.

WYOMING AT A GLANCE

Helmet Law	Partial	Exhaust Noise	No
Eye Protection	Not required	Earphones	Okay
Permit Restrictions	Yes	Checkpoints	No
Insurance	25/50/20	Automated Enforcement	No
Reciprocity	Yes	School Buses	Yes
Handlebar Height Restriction	Yes	Pedestrians	Yes
Daytime Headlight Use	Required by law	Move-Over Law	Yes
Left Lane Restriction	None	Excessive Speed Sanctions	No
Unchanging Traffic Signal Law	None	Mandatory Tow	No
Turn Signals	Not required	Feet Down	No
License Plate Display	Yes	Erratics	None
Fenders	Not required		

For more detailed information on the above, see next page or reference Chapter 2: U.S. Motorcycle Laws and Regulations.

WYOMING LAWS IN DETAIL

Wyoming does not use a demerit points system for tracking moving violations. If you rack up four convictions for moving violations such as speeding in a year, your license will be suspended for 90 days. Each additional violation within that one-year period will get you an additional 90 days. Suspensions are based on the date of the offense, not of the conviction. A reckless driving conviction will get you suspended for 90 days. Do it twice in five years and the suspension is for six months; a third time will probably get you revoked.

Getting nicked for less than 5 mph over in a 55- or 60-mph zone will not go on your driving record. Traveling less than 80 mph in a 65- or 75-mph zone will not go on your driving record.

HELMET LAW: Riders and passengers under 18 are required to wear helmets.

PERMIT RESTRICTIONS: A rider on a motorcycle permit may not carry passengers.

HANDLEBAR HEIGHT RESTRICTION: Handgrips must fall below shoulder height while the operator is seated.

LICENSE PLATE DISPLAY: Plates and tabs must be free of dirt and affixed to the bike so the numbers and letters are plainly visible and legible at all times.

EQUIPMENT REQUIREMENTS: A left-side rearview mirror is required, as are a passenger seat and footrests if carrying a passenger.

GOOD RESOURCES

Wyoming Department of Transportation: www.dot.state.wy.us
Wyoming State Statutes: http://legisweb.state.wy.us

INDEX

ABOUT THE AUTHOR

PAT HAHN is a motorcycle safety expert specializing in communications. He was raised in Illinois, spent 20 years in Minnesota, and currently lives on the West Coast. He's been a motorcycle safety instructor for 15 years and public information officer for the last 11. He is currently a motorcycle safety communications and outreach manager in Corvallis, Oregon.

Pat serves as the communications chair of the national association of State Motorcycle Safety Administrators (SMSA). He's also a member of the National Highway Traffic Safety Administration's technical assessment team and has conducted motorcycle assessments in Colorado, Ohio, Florida, California, North Carolina, and Massachusetts.

Pat holds a BA degree in communications and has written three books on the topic of safe riding: the advanced mental strategies book *Ride Hard, Ride Smart*, the beginner's book *How to Ride a Motorcycle*, and the advanced riding skills book *Maximum Control*.

Pat learned to ride the hard way: on his own, on a bike way too big and powerful for him, in downtown Chicago. Since then, he's worked hard to hone skills and strategies to be a better, safer rider and help others do the same. He uses a 1999 Honda VFR for commuting, entertainment, and touring. His wife, Kristin, and four-year-old son, Carl, live with him in the Cascadian wonderland that is the state of Oregon.